ENGLISH SPEAKING PEOPLE

AND

GLOBALIZATION

Alan B. Potter

Note for Librarians: A cataloguing record for this book is available from Library and
Archives Canada at www.collectionscanada.ca/amicus/index-e.html
ISBN 1-4251-0377-4

Offices in Canada, USA, Ireland and UK

Book sales for North America and international:
Trafford Publishing, 6E–2333 Government St.,
Victoria, BC V8T 4P4 CANADA
phone 250 383 6864 (toll-free 1 888 232 4444)
fax 250 383 6804; email to orders@trafford.com
Book sales in Europe:
Trafford Publishing (UK) Limited, 9 Park End Street, 2nd Floor
Oxford, UK OX1 1HH UNITED KINGDOM
phone +44 (0)1865 722 113 (local rate 0845 230 9601)
facsimile +44 (0)1865 722 868; info.uk@trafford.com
Order online at:
trafford.com/06-2134

10 9 8 7 6 5 4 3 2

TABLE OF CONTENTS

There are no footnotes and no end-notes.

There is no index except for the first page number of each chapter. If you wish to refresh your memory, please re-read the entire chapter.

ENGLISH SPEAKING PEOPLE AND GLOBALIZATION

Introduction

At the present stage of human development it is not possible to define globalization precisely. It is a term used generally to describe progress towards one world; an ever deeper economic integration; a common means of communication; compatible laws; and a reduction in the power of the nation state to restrict the freedom of expression and movement across borders. Since no single state can deal effectively with world-wide threats such as global warming or terrorism, cooperation is necessary if we want to survive.

But many people oppose these trends, especially when questions are raised concerning national sovereignty and the preservation of national languages.

The primary purpose of this book is to reduce irrational differences of opinion concerning globalization, what it means today and what it will probably mean in the future. You do not want to be on the wrong side in a war, especially in defence of misunderstandings which may be purely verbal.

This is a discussion between people who are already English speaking. It may be in the self-interest of other people to learn English as well as their own languages but they will not learn English until they have independently decided that they want to. We have the great advantage of already speaking it.

Governments have little control over that situation and many people in Europe are already more than capable of conducting their business affairs in English. How they converse with their families and friends at home is no concern of anyone else and is certainly not relevant to any of the controversial topics presented in this book. The English language is in the process of becoming a universal language so rapidly that no other languages can possibly compete with it. We are not considering an H.G. Wells prediction. It is something occurring today in China, Japan, India and South East Asia, as part of the natural drive to create additional wealth on an unprecedented scale.

But there is a factor other than language which has a greater impact for many individuals and that is fear of the future. Minorities are afraid that as other people become better off they must themselves become worse off. In self defence they may strongly resist globalization and not only in the economic context.

Fear of change is deeply embedded in the human psyche and originally must have been part of the survival instinct. Is that still the case today? The answer is that it need not be. We are not personally living in daily fear of a tsunami or of another Hurricane Katrina which would be far more devastating than the transition from one industry to another, for example. We must re-examine all of our basic assumptions to avoid irrational fears.

Abide with me is a hymn which is still sung frequently in churches on solemn occasions. One verse summarizes the nineteenth century philosophy in England very well:

Change and decay in all around I see
O Thou who changest not abide with me.

The possibility of change for the better was not considered. God cannot change for the better because he is already perfect. For mankind there seemed to be little hope for improvement, at least in this world.

However, in present day circumstances it is not rational to be pessimistic. Globalization has already increased the prosperity, health and social well-being of millions of people world wide. And globalization is in a comparatively early stage of development, particularly as we do not yet have the advantages of a common language.

The first six chapters of this book present a review of English as a language like no other. They should be read slowly and dispassionately to permit all existing preconceptions to be reconsidered. We can then proceed step by step through the arguments for and against globalization, on the assumption that our own English language will make everything possible.

That, at least, is the case presented by this book. We must all think it through very carefully from first principles.

Please Note:

The cover of this book shows the world as an oblate spheroid, slightly flattened at the poles.

The terms left and right do not mean much any more but the cover places England on the extreme left and America on the extreme right. That permits Australia, New Zealand, South East Asia and China to take centre stage.

That is how it should be.

———∞———

CHAPTER ONE

THE ENGLISH LANGUAGE

No one can say with certainty how language originated but we can suggest a reasonable hypothesis. A prehistoric family may have decided to build a wall and very soon used all of the rocks in the immediate vicinity of the cave. When the hunter returned empty handed it would be natural for his wife to emit a loud cry, to remind him to carry in some more rocks. The sound would of course have to be differentiated from other forms of warning.

Now let us suppose that the cave-man frequently brought in unsuitable rocks. Rather than collect the stones herself, the wife might vary the sound according to the stage her work had reached. Eventually, the man might learn that one sound meant 'large'; another 'round and flat'. For decorative work it would be necessary to invent noises for 'small', 'white', and so on.

This is not a very convincing example because the occasions might not have been sufficiently numerous but we can imagine that constantly repeated situations could become identified by different sounds.

It should be noted that the object need never be defined precisely. It is only required to use descriptive sounds to the extent necessary for sufficiently accurate identification. As soon as a stone has been chosen which is acceptable to the wife and which corresponds with what the husband thought the sound meant, there is no point in using any additional words. Language 'works' when the degree of definition is adequate for the immediate practical purposes.

That was the case before the development of written languages and remains the case for the great majority of verbal communication to this day. It is true also of the different pronunciations of each word. Widely divergent pronunciations may be correctly interpreted by all English speaking people and for that matter by foreigners learning our language. Our ancestors became good communicators by listening to other people, on the stage and in real life, and repeating words using the same pronunciation or something close to it. They knew the words before they wrote them down. For many centuries they did not need to know about an alphabet or spelling problems.

That was just as well because the English language was constantly changing, as four invasions brought in new words, new pronunciations and wider contacts through trade, commerce and international relations. By the beginning of the sixteenth century the process had stabilized to the extent that educated people could understand each other and communicate with each other in writing, more or less throughout the British Isles. However, that was a very small minority. The written language did not become widespread until the nineteenth century when elementary education was offered to the entire population.

Schools recruited teachers who had been brought up speaking the same dialects as their students. Problems of pronunciation and spelling arose in each district but children did learn to read and write. The words presumably formed in their heads in a way which reproduced mentally the pronunciation they used in speech. It is not surprising that local dialects persisted, and remain common to this day, up to a certain level of education. People living in Newcastle in England can hardly understand people living in Liverpool, for example. They rarely meet or feel the need to communicate, except as opponents at football matches. Verbal communications should always be referred to as spoken languages, in the plural. That is not the case with the written language in each country, which at least attempts to avoid controversy and to be all things to all people. But no national literature can be printed in books or published in newspapers in local dialects. There are simply too many of them to make printing and distribution worthwhile.

The fortunate students who went to university and studied academic literature tended to lose their local vocabulary and accents. That was often interpreted as a betrayal of their origins but it would not have been possible for all dialects, words and grammatical practices to survive in the written language. The spoken dialects must be preserved by people who wish to speak them as they learned them and as they exist at present.

Naturally, as writing developed there were many variations in spelling, even among the most educated members of each group of communicators. Not until Dr. Johnson wrote his dictionary could authors use the spelling which was most likely to be recognized and understood. It is not surprising that the Pilgrim Fathers continued to use some of the older versions which became discarded in England. The question of spelling does not arise until there are communications between people who have been educated in a common written language.

The complexities of English spelling and pronunciation cause many people to suppose that the rules are irrational or that there are no rules. Correct forms of writing and speech must be learned by rote at school and subsequently by the bitter experience of being corrected in public. Fortunately, once we have learned the words we do not forget them and rarely make a mistake. We are greatly assisted by the fact that there are indeed many rules of spelling, though they may be only dimly perceived and frequently ignored. We have learned to live with the difficulties because the flexibility of English offers tremendous advantages over all other languages.

The Chinese script allows not only different dialects but different language groups to communicate in writing but there is no prospect of replacing our alphabet by pictograms.

In the spoken language, several words may be pronounced identically which convey different meanings without presenting much danger of misunderstanding.

The meaning of each word is usually clear from the context and can be checked as necessary in the give and take of conversation. In writing, on the other hand, two words with different meanings can cause confusion if they are not visibly different.

It is true that some words meaning different things are spelled the same and are pronounced the same, such as mine (a possessive pronoun) and mine (an underground location). When such words frequently presented problems we may suppose that the spellings would be changed, and many were.

That is the reason for the vagaries of English spelling, as they are often called. They make the language more difficult to learn initially but they deal with major problems in writing which had to be solved before the language could be standardized.

Inventing new ways of spelling to provide visible differences in written words of course increased the problems of pronunciation and of teaching children to read, write and speak with each other. Linguistically we are always between a rock and a hard place: we are resistant to change yet we wish to support changes which appear most likely to assist the world to communicate more effectively. Progress is always slow but in the English language it has been sure and highly adaptive.

In spite of all the problems, English is the language of Shakespeare, Milton and The King James Bible; it ushered in the Enlightenment; and it is still capable of communicating philosophy, science and information systems to all who want to study them. No language has absorbed words and ideas from other countries as English has done and is still doing.

Why is English the best hope we have of developing a common written language world-wide? The answer is to be found in a re-examination of many of our assumptions and beliefs concerning English spelling, pronunciation and capacity for growth.

——— c⁄o———

ENGLISH SPELLING

Irish, Scottish, Gaelic, Breton and Welsh are closely related languages derived from prehistoric people in Western Europe, conveniently labelled as Celts. A common origin for all of them is generally agreed to be Sanskrit, which has clear affinities with Greek and Latin, as well as Persian. In Europe today we have a common Indo-European ancestral language with many branches including English. The so-called Celtic languages remained isolated and separate from English for many centuries but the English speaking people absorbed words from all sources and naturally grew much faster.

Most western countries use the same alphabet. It is derived mainly from Latin and the preceding alphabets of the ancient Greek, ancient Semitic and Phoenician languages. It is a long time since any letter was added to the English alphabet and somehow we have produced our entire written language using twenty-six letters.

As new situations arose which needed to be described and explained, and as new products and notions were developed which required names, there was never any problem in finding a combination of letters which would fill the gap. Rather the contrary; many different words were invented in different localities when only one was needed. English speaking nations never created a single authority which could enforce the adoption of one form rather than another or forbid an adoption which people found pleasing. Instead of a process of decision-making, changes were adopted as a result of trial and error, which took place over many years. That was fortunate because first thoughts are not always best. The development of the English language has been democratic rather than authoritarian.

Shakespeare handed out parts to his actors, not the complete play. That was the only way to protect a copyright in those days. Shakespeare was careless in the matter of spelling. He told the actors what his words meant and how to pronounce them, so his spelling did not matter. The plays were not printed until after his death. Perhaps he had given some of the complete plays to trusted friends and then they collected as many original versions as they could, all in Shakespeare's handwriting.

When they began to compose the First Folio they were faced by the tremendous problem of spelling. All printers had to decide how to spell each word and then keep to it throughout each publication. First they had to settle on how to spell Shakespeare's name. Eminent authorities to this day omit the final E, which shows that minor variations are not important as long as the meaning is clear. But everyone accepted the desirability of standardized spelling.

The predecessor languages contained many words which sounded the same, or almost the same; and many words which designated the same things but with completely different spellings and pronunciations. Choosing the most appropriate words to bring into the language was challenging enough. Then came the choice of spelling which would best differentiate the words from each other in the mind of the reader. Pronunciation was a secondary consideration and sometimes would be ignored altogether. The objective was to develop a written language which would be interpreted correctly and consistently throughout the British Isles. How that language would be spoken in different parts of the country was a matter of comparative indifference to the printers and linguistic scholars. They were wrestling with the difficulty of conveying ideas from one mind to another by writing, and without the possibility of clarification by speech.

Step by step, and over several centuries, they all came to the same conclusion. We must make the words look different. Wherever possible, we must vary the spelling. Only then will people be able to read rapidly without an appreciable pause to identify each word.

The first obvious decision was to preserve the spelling of the most important words derived from previous civilizations, however different they may seem in more recent languages; in fact, the more different the better. All of the scholars knew Greek and Latin so they did not need any persuading.

Philo means love of, hence philosophy, love of wisdom. Phobia means fear of, hence hydrophobia and anglophobes as opposed to anglophiles. Such prefixes and suffixes eg. pro, contra, pan, uni are valuable in preserving derivations and providing words which are instantly recognizable.

Another way to increase the number of words without affecting pronunciation is to combine vowels and consonants to produce the same sounds as other words but with different meanings, for example vain, vane, vein; rain, rein, reign; meet, mete, meat; I, eye, aye; rode, road, rowed; so, sow, sew; to, too, two; for, fore, four. There are thousands of such words and part-words. They may create some difficulties in conversation but in writing they are usually not confused.

More new words were made possible also by combining consonants and vowels to produce new sounds altogether. The addition of ING to a verb indicates the present participle. It also provides the sound for words like ring, bring and sing. Combining both sounds presents no problem to the reader, for example singing.

The letter H can be used to harden a G, as in ghost. But that is used so rarely that GH can be used in combination with vowels to produce the same vowel sounds but with different spellings, such as sight, might, right, instead of site, mite, rite. GH can also be used simply to confirm how the vowel should be pronounced, as in sigh, and it can replace the sound of F, as in laugh, cough, and rough.

Once the usefulness of GHT had been demonstrated it became widely used to make words look different, in combination with vowels other than i and with different consonants. Such elongated words cannot be confused with words without additional consonants, however rapidly we read.

An even more effective way of adding to the different ways of spelling is to add a consonant which is rarely used anywhere else to a word, wherever it cannot be pronounced. Adding a K to night changes the meaning completely. You cannot confuse the two words when reading, nor can you confuse no and know. The addition of other syllables to form the words knowledge and acknowledgements, does not mean that we can drop the silent K. Once you have used a silent letter in any word you must keep it for all subsequent words derived from it, otherwise chaos.

The silent K changes not to knot, which has a completely different meaning when you read it. B also crops up from time to time as a silent letter. When we plumb the depths we know it has nothing to do with plums.

H in the middle of a word may be aspirated very slightly or not at all without giving offence to anyone, whether educated or not. The H is not there to help with pronunciation but to differentiate words with different meanings; wile, while; wen, when; wear, where: why and the River Wye. We must identify the words as we read them and not pause to wonder which is witch.

G also can change a meaning without affecting the pronunciation; for example sign. By adding another syllable we form the word signal. It could not easily be pronounced sign – al, so we pronounce the G. But in gnat we do not pronounce the G. The pronunciation is a matter of common sense.

A double S followed by ION is pronounced SH. Admission pronounced admiss-i-on would add another syllable and would not be easy on the ear.

Words ending in IAL are also sometimes pronounced SHAL as in martial, and sometimes not, as in menial. L can also be silent as in would, to differentiate it from wood. Could and should also contain a silent L because they are related to would in meaning.

Health and wealth are interesting words. Heal means to make well, and people referred to the common weal, meaning the well being of the community. The scholars could have spelled the words helth and welth but they wanted to preserve the derivation. Similarly with stealth. If you read stelth you would not think of stealing.

Now you get the idea. There is a reason for everything.

Americans dropped the U from colour, vapour, honour and so on. At least Mr. Webster, did so. But he did not drop the H from honour, even though it is silent. Honor is an important word for Americans. They would never consider replacing it with a new phonetic spelling such as onner.

Americans usually decide not to fix what ain't broke. If words work, why change them? It is a pity they do not always accept their own advice. There is challenge enough to absorb new words into the language from sporting activities, economic developments, science and sociology from all over the world. The only requirement when inventing new words or new spelling is to make them noticeably different from the existing words in writing and printing. The reader must be able to recognize them immediately and consider the context, as well as the sound in his head which is how he thinks the word would sound when pronounced by him in conversation. He may be mistaken but that does not affect his understanding of the meaning of the words.

Once that simple fact is accepted, there is no limit to the number of words we can absorb. We can usually identify the meaning and pronunciation of words as soon as we see them written down. Spelling is not the problem; spelling is the solution to the problem. That is the supreme achievement of the English language. Our spelling is not abominable. It is a triumph of the human imagination as far as the written language is concerned.

CHAPTER THREE

—ols—

ENGLISH PRONUNCIATION

The word pronunciation is used in three different ways. The first refers to the spoken language. Individuals exchange questions and information to their mutual satisfaction. They reach agreement or they disagree about the subject of their conversation but, however far apart their views may be, they do not blame it on their pronunciation.

Every language contains dialects which survive in the different regions which contributed to the formation of a standard language. In some cases the differences are slight and in some others people can hardly understand each other, though they may live in villages on opposite sides of a mountain. They do not mind if they are not understood by people they never meet nor do they particularly care what other people read or discuss or argue about. Certainly they are not asking us to develop a phonetic alphabet for them. They would never need to learn it.

Local people understand each other because they were brought up together and pronounce words in the same way they have always done since they were children. They do not happily accept correction by people outside the group. In some cases they revel in the privacy which their dialect provides. People are usually proud of their dialects, which represent the extreme form of democracy in the development of language. The only people who can change them are the people using the dialects. And why should anyone want to change the way they speak? They are not doing any harm to anyone else.

The second use of the word pronunciation applies to the written language as a means of mass communication. When writing is read aloud to a large public it is necessary to pronounce the words in a way which is understandable to everyone and which will be interpreted in much the same way by people from many different backgrounds. That will only be possible when all of the listeners have a good vocabulary and do not themselves speak in incomprehensible dialects. We should not forget that we all go to the same plays, and have done so since before the Globe Theatre opened on the south bank of the Thames.

The problems of listening and correctly interpreting verbal messages have become more important with the development of radio, television and cinema. But the broadcasters of the mass media do not themselves speak dialects, or anyway not more than one. Broadcasters use something close to standard English, or standard American or standard Australian, Canadian or whatever form of speech is considered to be most acceptable to their listeners. Pronunciation changes according to fashion, and to some extent differently in each country, so there is nothing immutable about pronunciation. It would seem reasonable to conclude that there is nothing right or wrong about it.

For many years the British Broadcasting Corporation persevered with the speech it considered to be correct but finally gave way to the public demand for incorrect but popular dialects.

Dictionaries attempt to provide guidance but they are difficult for most people to understand. Native English speakers look up the meaning and spelling of words and then pronounce them as they please – until someone better informed corrects them.

Pronunciation is of course a learning tool. We have to start somewhere so we start with the alphabet. Children must be taught how to pronounce the letters of the alphabet and subsequently the words which will form the basis of their language skills. That educational process brings with it an understanding of the complexities of the language and sometimes the reasons for what appears to be our irrational spelling.

When we were first taught to read and write we were told that there are five vowel sounds. Later it became clear that every letter in the alphabet can be pronounced in more than one way. Even more disturbing would have been the realisation that many letters of the alphabet are often not pronounced at all, but are used to change the spelling of words, the better to recognise them in print, or to change the pronunciation of other letters. Teachers perhaps thought the bad news should be broken gradually if in fact we were expected to think consciously about it at all.

Then came five or ten years of seeing homework come back covered in red ink. Twenty spelling mistakes on each page. English students who were not fortunate enough to have a conscientious teacher or parent would be lucky to find any form of gainful employment. So many thousands of words and so much mystery in how they should be spelled and pronounced.

The difficulty of the English alphabet in the matter of pronunciation did in fact produce a widespread demand to do something about it. If a phonetic language could be developed, each symbol would be pronounced in one way only, thus differentiating words primarily by sound. It is supposed that the use of phonetics would make the language easier to teach and communication would be more accurate both in the written and the spoken forms of the language.

Nothing has come of the search for phonetic purity and for very good reasons. The problem is not at all that the different dialects made communication difficult at the conversational level. The difficulty was to convert the thousands of old words from the early dialects, and the thousands of new words, into an acceptable written form. Efforts to preserve the unity of the spoken and written languages were doomed to failure because there had never been any unity to preserve.

Young people today are inclined to develop new dialects of their own, perhaps to demonstrate their independence of mind. They may have no more concern for intelligibility or derivation than Lewis Carroll did in Jabberwocky. It must also be admitted that they have no objection to hearing and using words which would have been frowned upon at the Court of King Arthur. But good luck to them.

There is a third meaning of the word pronunciation if we use it to describe what happens when we are reading silently. We read so rapidly that we absorb entire phrases without mouthing or even thinking of individual words. We may assume that our personal pronunciation when reading silently is the same as everyone else but we do not know that unless we check with other people verbally. That makes it difficult to compare our reactions to old fashioned poetry which is in rhyme and metrical. But that perhaps does not matter very much if we do not enjoy reading old fashioned poetry.

CHAPTER FOUR

———ᐤᑌᐤ———

PHONETICS

In the preface to Pygmalion, George Bernard Shaw explains why he wrote the play:

"The English have no respect for their language and will not teach their children to speak it. They spell it so abominably that no man can teach himself what it sounds like. It is impossible for an Englishman to open his mouth without making some other Englishman hate and despise him. German and Spanish are accessible to foreigners; English is not accessible to Englishmen."

The rest of the preface is a powerful presentation of the need for an energetic phonetic enthusiast:

"That is why I have made such a man (Professor Higgins) the hero of a popular play".

Shaw subsequently directed the film which made the term phonetics familiar to the British public. Many years later the musical My Fair Lady did the same thing in North America. Few plays or musicals have been more popular or more misunderstood.

Professor Higgins wrote down conversations outside the Covent Garden Opera House which the people in the street had to agree were remarkably accurate. He used his own form of shorthand which reproduced pronunciation exactly. Higgins could tell where each person came from in London by listening to Cockney accents and middle and upper class accents. For what purpose?

Shaw was sympathetic with working class pronunciations and cultures. Perhaps he wanted all of the English dialects preserved and made part of our written language. At least one can only assume that is why he demanded a phonetic alphabet. Unfortunately, the speeches in Pygmalion and in My Fair Lady went all in the opposite direction. The first direct communication of Professor Higgins to Eliza Doolittle, the Cockney flower girl, was far from sympathetic:

"A woman who utters such depressing and disgusting sounds has no right to be anywhere – no right to live. Remember that you are a human being with a soul and the divine right of articulate speech; that your natural language is the language of Shakespeare and Milton and the Bible; and don't sit there crooning like a pigeon."

Perhaps after all Shaw did not wish to preserve dialects which were difficult for other people to understand. He wanted to educate them into the written language and to provide them with the opportunities which were available to everyone who could speak standard English.

The reference to bad spelling (a nightmare, as we have frequently been reminded) must of course apply to a written language. The dialects and pronunciation which cause Englishmen (not, fortunately, North Americans) to hate and despise their fellow men, can only apply to a spoken language. We all teach our children to speak by

pronouncing the spoken language as we speak it ourselves. We cannot teach them verbally in any other way.

That is the trouble with Shaw's statement that
Englishmen will not teach their children to speak the language. They do, but for Shaw it is the wrong language.

Let us suppose that there will always be people who
cannot write or read sophisticated literature or who do
not choose to do so. Why should they not converse and
pronounce words and communicate with their friends
and acquaintances on whatever basis they choose? We
are not there to listen to them or to correct them or to record their conversations. We read and write because that
is what we want to do and there is no reason to consider
ourselves superior beings on that account.

If, in spite of appearances, some people do in fact
want to discard their dialects they can easily do so. There
would be no need to preserve their present way of speaking. They could move into the society of people who
speak differently and leave their dialects behind. And
that is exactly what Professor Higgins persuaded Eliza
Doolittle to do in his play. Shaw had no problem in writing Cockney parts for actors and actresses who had never
lived in London. He did not need a phonetic alphabet nor
in fact did he use one. He repeated words and phrases
again and again as parents do. Professor Higgins taught
Eliza to speak correct English, not to read or write it.

Many famous authors reproduced local accents before Shaw, including Shakespeare, Dickens, Mark Twain
and many others. They all used English letters as Shaw

did in Pygmalion. He did not need a phonetic language unless he wanted to preserve the status quo of spoken languages.

All of the evidence is that Shaw was ambivalent on the subject of upward mobility. Professor Higgins was proud of his ability to take any girl from the slums of London and transform her into a duchess. Shaw confirmed that he approved of this result:

"Finally, and for the encouragement of people troubled with accents that cut them off from all higher employment, I must add that the change wrought by Professor Higgins in the flower girl is neither impossible nor uncommon. But the thing has to be done scientifically or the last state of the aspirant may be worse than the first."

By "scientifically" Shaw meant by means of phonetic symbols. But upward social mobility has been common for centuries without additions to the English alphabet. That is the answer to the advocates of phonetic spelling who want us all to use the same symbol for the same sound whenever it occurs. We simply do not need it.

Phonetic spelling would not remove the problems which arise when two words with different meanings are pronounced the same. To avoid all possibility of misunderstanding it would still be necessary to discard one of them and replace it with another symbol which would be pronounced differently. There are thousands of such words. We would have to invent new words for more than half of the language. And then pronounce them consistently using phonetic symbols which would be strange to everyone. No matter how abominable our spelling may seem to be, our last state would certainly be worse than our first.

And even if we succeeded, how long would the new purity last? Not long, unless we somehow cured all English speaking people of the inventiveness they have always shown.

It is amazing that Shaw did not realize the extent of the problem. He left all of his money to pursue an impossible objective. The English courts eventually declared his will null and void because nothing was being achieved by implementing the Shavian recommendations.

We are not as intelligent as Shaw but we absorb an incredible number of apparently irrational spellings like mother's milk. We are all much more clever than we are usually taught to believe.

The Greek sculptor, Pygmalion carved an ivory statue of a girl so beautiful that he fell in love with her. Assisted by Aphrodite she came alive in Pygmalion's arms. Whether or not they lived happily ever after is not mentioned in Greek mythology. In the sequel to his play, Shaw stated specifically that Professor Higgins was too old and too sophisticated to fall in love with Eliza. And Eliza was far too intelligent to waste her new-found freedom looking after Professor Higgins. Hollywood preferred a more romantic denouement. But under no circumstance could Eliza go back to her original spoken language and marry a man who was hated and despised by other Englishmen. She was doomed to adjust her way of life and presumably learn to read and write.

It is the written language which survives, not the ten thousand dialects which have been left behind. There can be no unity between the written and the spoken language, and we may as well admit it.

The genius of Shaw is not that he was always right but that he made us think. Long may Niagara on the Lake continue with the Shaw Festival.

_____ ✿ _____

CHAPTER FIVE

ZED OR ZEE

The one indisputable fact about pronunciation is that the last letter in the alphabet is not pronounced in America as it is in England. Why zed became zee is lost in the mists of time and why Z was pronounced zed in the first place is also a puzzle. The consolation is that the other twenty-five letters were retained, more or less, in the English tradition. If the entire alphabet had been re-designed we could hardly have claimed to have a common language.

Saying zee or saying zed does not make much difference to its usefulness but raises the question why we needed a twenty-sixth letter at all.

S is pronounced as a hard sound if there is an E somewhere in the word, as for example in choose, demise, dies, flies, ties, disguise, denies, phrase, rise, requires, supplies, wise.

But there is no e in is, his, busy, cousin, plays, pains, grows, prays, stays, and many others (including the word others). Even if there are some rules, we do not know them. Such is the computer which we call our brain that we almost never misspell them or mispronounce them. Why then did we need a Z?

At the beginning of a word the S is always soft as in soft. To make the first letter of a word a hard S sound seemed so important that the scholars included Z in the alphabet, for use in words such as zeal.

There is no word jeal but there is a jealous, pronounced jellous. It is much better to be zealous pronounced zellous. Ignore the pronunciation problems for the time being. The scholars could not deal with everything at once.

Z is never silent but it greatly increases the number of ways in which words can be spelled. Words containing a hard Z and a soft S could hardly be spelled without it, for example zest or size.

In America the words recognize, organize, realize and patronize are always spelled with a Z, but almost everyone in England spells those words with an S, also globalisation and civilisation.

It is believed that English people do not like the letter Z and avoid it whenever possible. Who is to tell them not to? They spell prize with a Z to differentiate it from prise but in surprise the S comes back again.

A thief will prise open a door in order to obtain his prize, showing some degree of private enterprize.

Promise is pronounced by everyone with a short i and compromise with a long i, no need for compromize.

To make a noun into a verb, for example criticize, a Z is usually acceptable but not for the hard s in criticism, spasm or of course, atheism and all other isms. We are not likely to make the mistake of writing about communizm.

Using C to produce a soft S could theoretically have led to the elimination of S altogether, using Z to produce all of the hard S sounds. That is the phonetic dream of two symbols which could never be confused verbally. But the written language requires much more flexibility than that.

We have the 26 letters of our alphabet and that is all we need, in England, America and throughout the world. All we have to do is learn how to use them in writing. Pronunciation is a matter of individual taste and English speaking people nowadays have no problem with that.

CHAPTER SIX

———o◦o———

NUMBERS

Numbers are symbols which were invented before spoken words. In very early times they were used by traders to facilitate barter, before the invention of money.

We can imagine a Phoenician trader loading pots of olive oil into his ship in Italy. For every pot he drew a short vertical line on parchment. After four lines he drew a line through them, meaning five. He could then rapidly total the number of groups and reach agreement with the supplier. No doubt the supplier counted with his fingers as the pots passed out of his hands. If he saw a pot being missed he would grab the trader's arm, or perhaps wag his finger at him. No words needed.

The same calculations would be made in Cornwall when the copper and tin were being loaded for Roman armour. Cuneiform writing looks very like that in the British Museum. And not only Arabic numbers. Roman numerals are just the same. You cannot do long division with them.

Symbols for numbers 1-12 came from India and via the Indo-European languages, from which eventually came the European and English words.

Why is one not wun? We do not know and it does not matter. Nothing we, or G.B. Shaw, could do would ever change it.

The Boy Scouts sing:

"One is one and all alone and evermore shall be so."

They mean that one is 1 and all alone, and so it is.

Why do we need words to describe numbers, which are the perfect symbols themselves? We can use numbers for dates, times, money and statistics no matter how many millions of units there may be. Of all the written words which might theoretically be reduced to basic sounds or pronounceable symbols, numbers are the best candidates. But it cannot be done.

Here is an odd turn of events. In conversation you cannot use numbers at all, only words. You could not easily indicate with your fingers a number exceeding ten. You cannot indicate approximate numbers like a dozen, a score or several hundred. Try to deal with space travel without using the word 'light-years'.

None is clearly a condensed form of not one. We could not spell that as nun because nuns were very important people in the Middle Ages and probably still are.

One is easy to turn into once. And once leads to twice and thrice. Very useful.

The word 'to' introduces the infinitive of all verbs in the language. It is used even more frequently than two so we give two a silent w. Too means as well, which is clearly different from to or two. The w in two was probably suggested by the German zwei.

The Boy Scouts sing:
"Three, three, the lily white boys
Clothed all in green-oh",
Some religious reference no doubt. We would not want to change three.

Four is used as much as any other number but not as frequently as the word for. Imagine a phonetic symbol which we had to use for both words. Which would we discard? And then what would we shout as a warning to golfers that we might not drive straight down the fairway?

Five describes the Roman V and we could easily call it V if we wanted to. But we do not.

In the spoken language we will always hear, or interpret, or remember numbers incorrectly from time to time. There is only one way to avoid such errors and that is to write the numbers down. Spoken numbers are essential but can hardly be binding among human beings, especially economists.

Seven has always been considered a magic number in religious history and mythology. It would be a pity not to be able to include it in conversation.

Eight shows how many years ago the scholars invented ght. They did not want a number ate. Eight is consistent with weight and freight but not with height, a fact which all scholars probably hate. Never mind. Eight fulfils all of our criteria for a verbal number. It cannot possibly be mistaken for anything else.

Nine is the most simple form of word in respect of spelling and pronunciation. Nin with an e makes the long i. In one of the predecessor languages nine is spelt nein, meaning no. If a Saxon speaking scholar was part of the group he must have been outvoted in respect of spelling but his associates accepted his recommended pronunciation.

Ten is also a simple piece of spelling and pronunciation. It could hardly be shorter unless perhaps the scholars considered calling it X, in the Roman manner. But ex already meant past or previous. You would not want your ex-wife to be known as your tenth wife.

Eleven is a mystery.

Twelve may be the approximate sound in ancient Hebrew of the number of disciples at the Last Supper. Why would we want to question such a prestigious word? We all learned to spell and pronounce twelfth after a few years of trial and error and would not want to switch to a symbol.

The other seven numbers are between twelve and twenty. Teen is a form of ten.

We can write down fractions in words if we really want to and we can refer to a simple decimal as two point-five. But arithmetic can only deal with numbers. Science needs mathematics and mathematicians are very different people from we readers and writers. We must have words; they must have numbers.

Now we can see that the problems with the alphabet and the spelling and verbal skills which we need to develop a written language and speak it intelligibly do not apply to numbers. There we have the complete reverse. Our numerical system is an international language. Mathematicians do not need to pronounce numbers at all. They write them down and work on them silently throughout their lives.

When non-mathematicians make mistakes with numbers they can easily be corrected. No one questions the judgements of qualified experts. Who can doubt that the world would be a better place if we could develop a common language accepted by all? That, it is suggested here, is the role that English can perform in the development of globalization, but only when the world is ready for it.

———cめ———

EUROPEAN HISTORY

Children are taught history, if at all, in their own language. In the limited time available it is natural for history teachers to concentrate on the history of their own language groups. Students everywhere learn different versions of history which tend to be ethnocentric and incompatible with globalization.

English students do not suffer from that defect to the same extent because their history involved all of the European nations and later, all countries of the world including their languages. People who learn English as a second language improve their communication skills and at the same time become capable of re-learning history. The history of England even before the Roman Empire was all in the direction of globalization, at least it seems so retrospectively.

From artefacts and clothing discovered in burial grounds it seems there was always movement between Europe and the British Isles. Individuals, families and tribes rowed over to explore and to trade and often settled on unoccupied farm land. Sometimes they drove off the Ancient Britons, whoever they were, and sometimes the immigrants were welcomed. Intermarriages no doubt reduced whatever animosity there had been initially. When the Romans were victorious in Europe the defeated tribes sometimes escaped to England. To persuade them not to rearm and return to the mainland as unbeaten enemies the Roman emperors ordered several invasions. Julius Caesar himself landed in 55 BC and 54 BC but did not stay very long. The 400 year occupation of Britain was initiated by Claudius in 43 AD.

The Roman legions did not march on for ever. They stopped at the River Rhine and at the borders of Scotland and Wales. They did not invade Ireland. They also stopped at the bottom of fortified hill towns in Europe – whenever there did not seem to be much point in going on.

The people in the unconquered areas were proud of their refusal to submit and of preserving their local dialects, religious beliefs and political history, such as it was. But they suffered in many ways compared with the inhabitants of the Roman Empire. They had no Latin language and no four hundred years of Pax Romana. When they could not fight Romans they fought each other. Today we would call it continuous tribal warfare.

However, that made them well qualified to invade peaceful countries when the legions returned to Rome to fight the enemies there. The Emperor Constantine could not drive them out and eventually moved his entire government, most of the army and the Catholic Church to Constantinople, presently Istanbul. Then there was no defence against the Saxons, Danes and Norsemen

(Northmen or Normans) who streamed down into Western France and subsequently across to England.

From the third century AD the Roman Empire was no longer considered to be impregnable. In AD 260 Dacia (the present day Romania) was invaded by Goths and was abandoned by Rome. In about 372 the Huns led by Attila defeated the Ostrogoths and settled in Hungary. The Visigoths under Alaric sacked Rome in 410 and moved into Gaul and Spain until they were conquered by the Moors in 711. The Ostrogoths moved west from Hungary until the Emperor Justinian reconquered Italy in 555. The Vandals crossed the Rhine in 406 and settled in Gaul and never left.

The people who did not speak Latin were known as barbarians. They were teutonic tribes from northern Europe and nomadic hordes from Asia. They brought their languages and cultures with them and they were warlike people. They did not want to associate with other tribes and never replaced the peace and civilization of the Roman Empire.

The tribes in Britain also refused to join each other and opposed the successive invasions but they fought losing battles. By 1066 they were more or less united under William the Conqueror, a Norman who always believed that he owned half of France. He and his court and aristocracy spoke Norman French for another four hundred years.

During that period the English tribes did not fight each other very much. They developed agriculture under the Manorial System and continued more or less happily under the government of the Norman monarchy. The first thing William did in England was to collect data from the farms, villages and towns concerning economic activities. The statistics still exist in the Domesday Book. Market towns and trade farther afield produced slowly but surely a common local language. It is called Middle English. You can still read it and perhaps understand it in The Canterbury Tales by Geoffrey Chaucer.

The English kings tried to return to their ancestral homes in France on several occasions, as recorded subsequently by Shakespeare. They succeeded and failed repeatedly and finally gave up because they became interested in exploration elsewhere in the world.

Before the Battle of Agincourt, Henry V encouraged his soldiers to defeat a much larger French army by speaking to them in English. After that the English court adopted English and gave up pretending that they were really French. Using Middle English, Norman French and all of the languages imported into England by the invasions and by international trade, Shakespeare and other Elizabethan dramatists developed the English we know today.

They and many other writers invented new words and wrote the best poetry and prose the world had ever known. Soon, the scholars began to write it all down and print it using the presses imported from Germany. They incorporated in it all of the religious, economic, political and scientific information which then existed. Most people could not read it but an increasing number could.

The mainland of Europe had a similar experience without such a happy conclusion. Agricultural and commercial activities developed at an even more rapid rate and the Roman ports and roads were renewed sufficiently to handle vast quantities of produce. Trade expanded and with it came prosperity; but with prosperity came increased military capacity, which ambitious individuals wanted to use for their own benefit. Emperors, kings and barons could do nothing to stop the process of self-destruction. More often than not they organized it. Either they were hoping to create an empire or trying to protect themselves from the empires built by others.

The large numbers of each language group which flooded into Europe thought they could be self-sufficient, as tribes have always done. But one thing they could not do, and persuaded themselves they did not want to do, was to develop a common language. That is what kept them apart and made them enemies. That is what still keeps many people apart today.

But language was not the only problem. The most significant historical factor in the Second Millennium was the development of the nation-state system. Europe divided itself into many countries separated by rigid boundaries, different languages and powerful armies. Disagreements followed by devastating warfare became the expected pattern of international relations. Every country in turn was defeated, occupied and stripped of assets. Nothing occupied their minds more than the dreams of revenge.

Throughout the 18th and 19th centuries England maintained a consistent foreign policy. The British Government invariably supported the second most powerful nation in Europe. That meant switching sides quite frequently and Europeans referred to England as Perfidious Albion. The determination to prevent any country from becoming the master of Europe of course involved England in every war, whether it was in the national interest or not. But English diplomatists did not want to be ruled by a master race. Somehow England did benefit and become the greatest economic and military power on earth.

But the nation states in Europe and elsewhere for some inscrutable reason refused to recognise that fact. They set about becoming empires of their own, around the periphery of the British Empire. They developed irreconcilable differences and an uncompromising determination to go their own way and they each believed they were powerful enough to do so.

There is no simple explanation of the great importance people attach to national ambitions, even in terms of self-determination and defence against aggression. From the oratory and aggrandizement of every government it could be supposed that states protect their citizens from foreign interference and malign intentions, and that legislators need take no account of the interests or desires of neighbouring countries. A nation-state is by definition a sovereign power, which means that it is not answerable to any higher authority.

These pretensions are so obviously false and self-contradictory that they can only be described as the wishful thinking of frightened people. In reality, the nation-state system creates unnecessary friction and accentuates the very dangers it is supposed to avoid. Twentieth Century political history can be summarized as the signal failure of European states to protect the people of the world from war and destruction on an ever increasing scale.

As one disaster succeeded another, one would have expected a general revulsion against nationalism and the policies which had so often ended in failure and tragedy. In 1918 there was indeed a widespread feeling that the world should be organized on a more rational basis, and again in 1945 a supranational authority was proposed. On each occasion, however, other counsels prevailed, apparently with the approval or at least the consent of the majority of the electorate in every state. All of the evidence indicated that no-one could make more calamitous mistakes in the conduct of foreign affairs than national governments, yet the system retained the support of all democratic and totalitarian regimes. There is apparently an infinite faith in the wisdom and benevolence of national leaders compared with any alternative which is thought to be foreign or supranational.

That is a remarkable phenomenon and obviously in need of explanation. Some states act comparatively sensibly; some are too small to arouse fear or animosity in others; and some have been too isolated to be seriously threatened or affected by external economic or political policies. But as the world shrinks in size, no country can safely assume that the irrational and self-destructive forces of extreme nationalism or religion will not reassert themselves.

In-group and out-group feelings can arise on any number of subjects but nothing separates people like different languages. When the nations of Europe had fought themselves to a standstill they discovered new trade routes, new populations overseas and new sources of disagreement. Again the conflicts were exacerbated by incomprehensible speech on both sides. And still the European tribes were sufficiently proud and self-confident to believe that they could survive and prosper without close collaboration with everyone else.

WWI and II were called world wars because they seemed to involve almost everyone in the world. But a better description would have been Global Wars because the future of global civilization depended on which side won. The soldiers of every army believed they were fighting for their country but English soldiers always thought they were fighting for the world. American soldiers had an even better reason for that, because America could have stayed out of European wars altogether. As things turned out, all countries in the world have the opportunity to proceed with globalization if they want to.

At the end of World War II there would have been widespread political and economic collapse without assistance from the United States. In the long term interest of the American people no doubt, policies and financial resources were provided on a tremendous scale and Europe recovered. America did not fight Germany or Japan to preserve the European empires but apart from that they did more for their allies who spoke different languages than had ever been provided before. Without nationalism, Europe would presumably have been eternally grateful.

International wars were followed by the threat of totalitarian enslavement world-wide in support of communist ideology. That too was defeated by the United States, almost single handed as far as military power was concerned. By the end of the Millennium the brotherhood of man appeared to be a distinct possibility. Everyone could get on with the creation and distribution of wealth, travel, Olympic Games, sports and entertainments of every conceivable kind, and the happy experience of bringing up their children in peace.

The European Union was formed and extended to include Eastern Europe with a population even greater than that of the United States. China moved strongly in the direction of free enterprise although it remained communist in name and still has a totalitarian government. All countries became more prosperous with an increasing expectation of life. They all seemed to be willing to assist everyone else in times of national disaster. Such was the glorious prospect as the Second Millennium came to an end.

So one might have thought, even though the world was still composed of separate sovereign states, incompatible religions and incomprehensible dialects. But suddenly the Twin Towers came crashing down.

"O what a fall was there my countrymen
When I and you and all of us fell down
And bloody treason flourished over us."

In this case it was not treason but what was it? We do not know. It seemed remarkably like a declaration of war, though no army had marched over the sacred boundary of a sovereign state. War could not be declared against an enemy because there was no-one to declare it against.

In 1939 the British Government declared war against Germany and nothing happened for almost a year. It was called the phoney war but everyone knew they were at war. There had never been a declaration of war which was subsequently withdrawn. Are the terrorists, whoever they are, likely to retract their determination to fight the infidels to the death?

Bin Laden thinks he is at war and so do his associates.

But do we?

CHAPTER EIGHT

—∾—

WAR

When defeated by the Romans people could lay down their arms and live in peace under the rule of law. No doubt there were unfortunate incidents from time to time but usually there was no mass slaughter of civilians. Generally speaking the occupying troops seem to have behaved surprisingly well.

That could not always be said of the Vikings, Saxons or Danes who came to England, but the Normans won outright and put down subsequent uprisings like the gentlemen they were.

That changed with the development of the nation-state system. Europeans fought to the death because they did not want to be governed by foreigners and sometimes with good reason.

The First World War was a sobering experience for everyone who took part in it. All of the participants except America joined the League of Nations and renounced war as an instrument of national policy. They signed disarmament agreements and made solemn treaties of non-aggression.

The trouble with those new year resolutions was that they convinced the villains that war would rapidly be

successful. The democracies were thought to be deca-
dent. Certainly many people in England were pacifists,
including the Labour Party and Oxford and Cambridge
universities. But it turned out that pacifism did not mean
surrender to invading armies. It expressed a fervent belief
that if we did not interfere with other people then they
would not interfere with us. Much turning of the other
cheek and hoping for the best, as many nations are still
doing in respect of Iran and Iraq, Syria and Lebanon.

An exception to the inter-war doctrine was the point
of view down-under. The Australians had seen tiny Japan
defeat mighty Russia in 1904 and sink most of its Pacific
Fleet within a few weeks. That was all the pacifism the
Australians wanted. After that they never needed a wake-
up call again and nor did New Zealanders.

When the bombs started to rain down in 1940 we did
not hear about pacifism any more. We did not want to
find ourselves speaking German or Russian or Japanese.
To say nothing of going to concentration camps or gas
ovens.

North Americans were even less pacifist but they
were convinced that Europeans periodically killed each
other and nothing could be done about it. The Middle
West in particular was strongly isolationist until Pearl
Harbour.

When the GI's marched into concentration camps in
Germany they could hardly believe their eyes. Nor could
anyone else. The photographs and films were flashed
around the world. Only then was it universally agreed

that the war had been unavoidable and that it had to be won if civilization was to survive.

When the German people came to their senses they believed it too. There is no previous case in history of a nation-state regretting anything. The Germans may now be the least tribal people on earth.

Poverty and the atomic bomb preserved world peace until communist North Korea invaded democratic South Korea. Civil war you might have thought. No, aggression! A United Nations vote in the absence of the USSR authorized the fight to a standstill by blue helmeted troops and N. Korea/China. Russia would never make that mistake again. All opposition to communist dictatorship after that was organized and mainly paid for by the United States, with some support from other democracies. The Vietnam War was strongly criticized as the wrong war in the wrong place at the wrong time but America and her allies did finally win the Cold War. That is to say, the Russian Empire collapsed and western civilization did not.

That brought us to the end of the Twentieth Century. Since then there have been many local massacres, religious conflicts, fierce tribal enmity, starvation and terrorism and no effective action to stop them by the United Nations.

It is not easy to establish who can possibly gain from this new era of violence or who can possibly think they will gain. Reading the news today is not much different from reading 14th Century history.

That does not mean we can behave like unconcerned spectators and let things take their course. After September 11th there was consternation but few expected America to do nothing.

The International Law of War and Peace is based on a thousand years of experience. A sovereign state can declare war against another state which has been recognized as sovereign by the community of nations. To declare that a state of war exists is a sovereign act. It does not need the agreement of the other party. States can pretend they are still at peace if they wish; but usually they take up the cudgels and defend themselves as best as they can. A declaration of war validates the laws concerning the treatment of prisoners and other humanitarian concerns, which is better than nothing.

But if there is no sovereign state to declare war against, war cannot be declared. That is the law. Organize a police action or stay at home. Suffer in silence in fact. Perhaps in future we must learn to accept the hard knocks of fate uncomplainingly but in 2004 the President and Congress of the United States of America decided they had had enough of Saddam Hussein.

As King Lear once said:

"I will do such things –
What they are yet, I know not – but they shall be
The terrors of the earth".

In other words, hit them back.

The British Government was sympathetic. In 1842 the British army decided to evacuate the 4,000 soldiers and their families from Kabul to safety through the Khyber Pass. The Afghan guerrillas slaughtered them to a man. One surgeon fell over a cliff and lived to tell the tale. No-one thought it was going to be easy to invade The Middle East.

The first problem that cropped up was the Arabic language and its many dialects. The CIA American personnel only spoke English. They could not recruit Arabic speakers who were loyal to America no matter how much they were paid. And if there were any CIA agents who could infiltrate the terrorist ranks they seem to have been rapidly liquidated. Elections held in Afghanistan for the first time may benefit the local population but they are not likely to result in victory over the terrorists or control over the worldwide distribution of opium without strong American support.

George Bush knew from his father that Saddam Hussein was unlikely to reform himself or his Sunni minority government nor correct his aversion to Shiites or Kurds and almost anyone not related to his immediate family or others not within his immediate tribe.

Here again the British Foreign Office had had invaluable experience. The British Government had been requested by the League of Nations to accept a mandate to govern Iraq and, based in Basra, did so for many years. It was supposed that if the British army returned in 2004 they would be welcomed with open arms. So they were but those arms had been provided by Iran. Expecting gratitude and economic privilege in respect of favours dating back to the British Empire proved to be have been somewhat optimistic.

Surely the United Nations Organization could agree that the government of Saddam Hussein should be replaced by an elected majority?

But the UN is an association of sovereign states whose majority believes in the inviolability of national frontiers, even though many in the Middle East were drawn by young British administrators using simple geometric formulae, mainly confined to straight rulers. In 1946 the Foreign Secretary of England and subsequent Prime Minister, Lord Eden, made the following statement in the House of Commons:

"If Hitler had stayed within his own borders we would have had no quarrel with him."

That was after Anthony Eden had been fully informed about the Holocaust. As the UN today includes members who would be happy to see a second holocaust, there was not much to be hoped for in New York.

George W. Bush decided to enter Iraq by force, be welcomed by the grateful citizens and hold elections under American surveillance. Congress supported him or at least did not initiate impeachment proceedings. There were reservations among both parties but no-one knew what else to do. Better do anything than nothing, it, was generally agreed. With any luck America would uncover weapons of mass destruction, identify the terrorists and unleash the potential energy of democracy.

Elections were indeed held in 2005 and a majority government will see what can be done with the Sunnis and the Kurds and Iran and the many terrorists factions. The Bush policy will be vindicated or we will all be wondering what should be done next. Certainly if results fall short of expectations we will not want to do that again and neither will America. We may suppose a century could go by of leaving people in the Middle East to their own devices but not if they acquire nuclear weapons and disrupt the Middle East politically and economically.

Even if the people of Iraq accept majority rule, they will still have to deal with the fact of terrorism and so will the rest of the world.

Part of the problem has been a reluctance to consider any possible limitation there may be to the political potential of democracy itself, for ourselves and other people. But of one thing there can be no reasonable doubt. We are at war in any common sense use of the term. The democracies must be prepared for the foreseeable future to use the armed forces to maintain law and order internally and externally.

The part to be played by the United Nations Organization becomes increasingly opaque. The members recognize each other as governments in control of a defined area and responsible for maintaining internal peace and good order. When it can clearly be seen that a state is not able to protect its citizens or defend its borders one would suppose that the other members would withdraw recognition from it; but they do not. They pick up sides, as they always did in the days of tribal warfare. In the matter of new ideas the nation state system is currently bankrupt. Other means of collaboration must be developed between men of good will.

---∞---

CHAPTER NINE

CANADA

In 1759 General James Wolfe defeated the French troops under the Governor of Quebec, the Marquis de Montcalm on the Plains of Abraham. In the following year the capture of Montreal by General Amherst, head of the British Army, put an end to the dream of a French empire in America.

Voltaire wrote Canada off as a few acres of snow but England did not see it that way. The Prime Minister, William Pitt the Elder, had given the highest priority to the conquest of Canada. He won the loyalty of the militia by an order which gave them equal rank with the royal officers in the field. That was a stroke of genius. It was the first sign that one day, far distant, the colonies of the British Empire might become self-governing. A century later it happened.

The French settlers had never been given any hope of equal treatment. They were expected to lay down their lives in the militia but all of the senior officers were French aristocrats. When they lost the war the aristocracy went home to France leaving the settlers to get on with the British as best they could. Montreal capitulated to General Amherst because he offered terms that seemed unexpectedly generous. The people who became known as French Canadians, estimated to be approximately 70,000 at that time, agreed to remain neutral in all future conflicts between Britain and France. In return they were allowed to practise the Roman Catholic religion; to appoint a Bishop for Quebec; to preserve the French system of civil laws; and to speak, write and read in the French language. Those terms were further extended in the Quebec Act of 1774. That agreement, so unusual in its time, has preserved French Canadian culture to this day.

After 1760 the settlers felt no loyalty to France nor were they bound to the culture of France, at least until comparatively recent times. In fact they felt that they had been very badly let down by France. They lost the war because the promised reinforcements never arrived. They had taken over the land along the St. Lawrence River, becoming subsistence farmers and later developed agricultural markets; and of course were the "coureurs du bois" and masters of the fur trade. They were the great explorers of the north of Quebec and of western territories north of Upper Canada, and had earlier explored mid-Western America to the Mississippi River. They soon had the opportunity to demonstrate their gratitude to the British Crown.

In 1775 the Americans decided to make a surprise attack on the British troops in Canada. They believed correctly that England intended to capture Boston and isolate the other colonies from Canada. It seems likely that Washington expected the Canadian settlers to join the American War of Independence with enthusiasm. The original secret expedition under General Benedict Arnold left New York with only 1000 men. He found that the Quebec settlers were prepared to put up a spirited resistance and withdrew. Later he was replaced by 3000 men under General Sullivan, still one would suppose an inadequate force.

The British troops and settlers in Upper Canada could well have been beaten but the French Canadians in Lower Canada resisted all attempts to enter Quebec. The American troops must have been astonished, first, that the English colonists were loyal to King George III; secondly that they were supported by the French habitants, and thirdly that they had been so badly beaten.

It is clear that without French Quebec the English Canadians would have been absorbed by the United States in total, or one province at a time, within a very few years. In 1812 President Madison declared war against England, though not supported by all of the states. Nevertheless his forces cleared Lake Ontario, captured Toronto, destroyed the British flotilla on Lake Erie and made themselves masters of Upper Canada. Once again their attack on Lower Canada was beaten back and a fresh advance of British forces and Canadian irregulars again recovered the Upper Province.

Subsequent threats of invasion could have been made, and offers to join America, which Canadians would have been foolish to refuse. But Canada with a defiant French speaking heartland was a different matter altogether, and still is. No other English speaking country has obligations to another language group written into its Constitution. How could Washington deal with the Quebec agreement? At all events, for whatever reason, Canada was left to its own devices.

After that there was little enmity between English and French Canadians. They had saved each other and could live together. They were kept distant from one another by the fierce determination of the French to keep their language. They were entitled to keep it so they kept it, and not only in their homes as the Welsh people did. The majority of French people in Canada saw no need to speak any thing else. The English and French Canadians became the "Two Solitudes", a description invented by Hugh MacLennan as a title to his famous book. They were not enemies. Their paths seldom crossed except in Montreal.

In the nineteenth and twentieth centuries the Canadian economy and infrastructure was developed primarily by English Canadians or more accurately perhaps by Scottish and Irish Canadians. The managers of banks and large corporations spoke English and so did their employees. It was not easy to put people to work who did not speak English, so those French Canadians who were ambitious were obliged to learn English and many did so. But they were not happy about it. The constitutional right to speak French was never in doubt but the economic environment was such that many people had no entry to government or business prosperity. Montreal was the financial centre of Canada but French people, being rurally based, remained an underclass in cities and towns.

Then in 1960 came the Quiet Revolution in Quebec. It resulted in additional legal protection for the French language in places of business and eventually to official bilingualism everywhere else in Canada. Many companies did not wish to force their employees to write all correspondence in French, including inter-office memos, and they moved their head offices to Toronto. It is estimated that 250,000, people including wives and families, moved to Ontario on that account.

But the companies and government offices which remained in Quebec did recruit and train and promote large numbers of French speaking Canadians now referred to as Québecois. So from the point of view of the French language and opportunity for the Québecois, the revolution was a success.

The Quebec economy, like all other provincial economies, exports at least half of its domestic production, and imports an even greater value of goods and services, both requiring continuous communication with other countries and provinces which are not French speaking. So the successful entrepreneurs and businessmen in Quebec do in fact speak and write in English for a substantial percentage of their time, and very effectively too. The productivity of Quebec fell for a time compared with Ontario but is now rapidly resuming its former supremacy in many areas of trade and commerce.

So, although there is presently a demand from a political party in Quebec, the Parti Quebecois, for independence from the rest of Canada it does not seem to be based on complaints about language or religion. What the Quebec electorate will decide we do not know. Anything can happen. But all Canadians, federally and provincially, could well consider the soliloquy of Richard of Gloucester in Shakespeare's Henry VI, Part III Act 2;.

> **Why, then, I do but dream on sovereignty**
> **Like one that stands upon a promontory**
> **And spies a far-off shore where he would tread**
> **Wishing his foot more equal with his eye**
> **And chides the sea that sunders him from thence**
> **Saying he'll lade it dry to have his way.**

———oↄ———

QUEBEC

Approximately half of the electorate of Québec Province is primarily French speaking and they are considering the possibility of taking on the trappings of national sovereignty. Call them the Parti Québecois – the P.Q.

The other half is either English speaking, or immigrants in other language groups, or French Canadians who do not want to separate from Canada. For the sake of convenience we will call them the Rest of Quebec.

This situation is remarkably similar to the division in the entire country between Quebec and the Rest of Canada. It is virtually impossible to change the Canadian Constitution without the unanimous agreement of all Provinces but Quebec may choose to ignore the Canadian Constitution and the Supreme Court of Canada, so determined is the P.Q. to become a sovereign power. If by any means that is what happens, the P.Q. will face exactly the same series of problems as the Canadian Government does at present from separatism.

All of the so-called sovereign governments of Europe as well as Quebec Province are threatened by the demographic fact of a birth rate below the replacement rate of 2.1 children per family. An aging population reduces the number of working population that supports pensions, health schemes and educational requirements of a country to say nothing of liberal and socialist governments with continuously increasing demands on the Gross National Product.

Quebec is also faced by a decline in the number of immigrants who want to speak a European language. The preference given to the French language by France has increased the number of immigrants from North Africa who unfortunately appear not willing to assimilate into the culture of France. Many of them have no business training or opportunity to move elsewhere and unemployment in France is the highest in Europe. The maintenance of law and order is threatened but France, the oldest, most inner-directed and most proud nation state in the world, at present has no solution to these problems.

What does the P.Q. think about immigration from French speaking countries? How will sovereignty help them if none of the Francophone countries has a culture compatible with the Québecois? Clearly the P.Q. will not welcome five million immigrants from North Africa simply because they speak French. If they had any such thought, France would happily supply them immediately. If nothing is done, of course, the supremacy of the French language in Quebec may be lost long before the end of this century, which is exactly what the P.Q. is trying to avoid. But how, without destroying the Quebec culture?

Then there are the economic questions. Will Quebec maintain or even increase its present tariffs, subsidies and business intervention? Will Quebec Inc. still be a vital component of economic stability? And will that mean customs officers and a border around Quebec, the largest state in North America? How much will that cost? Can we expect every Québecois to refrain from smuggling?

Will individual families, French and English, be permitted to leave with all their goods and chattels? Will corporations? Will some undesirable people be forced to leave?

Will America, or Canada for that matter, permit Quebec to negotiate trade terms without reference to subsequent exports from Quebec? Canada considers itself to be sovereign but that did not solve the soft wood lumber controversy with the USA.

And security from terrorism? Will Quebec be as independent as France and as ineffective? Any need for agreements with Canada or America?

There are many other challenges for a new government, internally and externally – all of which take time and money to negotiate and which may or may not be resolved in the interest of Quebec. Will Quebec have allies and diplomatic policies that have no relation to Canadian interests? Is it likely that a separate Quebec could govern itself decisively and effectively if the electorate is still divided between two equal and opposite parties? How would Quebec do better than Ottawa if it had minority governments or very small majorities?

Would the sovereign government of Quebec dispense with strict adherence to democracy, perhaps as a temporary measure? How would Canada and America take to that? Does outside opinion mean nothing to a sovereign state? And how much money will Quebec devote to its armed forces?

All these questions make it rather important to discuss in advance the Quebec Constitution as it is likely to be adopted by the P.Q. in the event of a referendum majority. Will it be a continuation of the British Constitution with or without a Governor-General? Or will it be an American type constitution with a President and separation of powers? Not, surely, a French constitution? Or will it be a completely original contribution to democratic government?

One would suppose that a majority would be more likely to vote for separatism if a draft constitution could be studied and approved in principle in advance. Perhaps the P.Q. elite have already thought about the proposal they will publish when they have agreement amongst themselves but it seems impossible that they already have a draft, which they have managed to keep secret. And why should they keep their thoughts to themselves? Why are they not proud of their views, whatever they may be? Perhaps they have not got that far in their hopes and dreams to want to risk antagonizing their supporters.

It is possible that the P.Q. have been watching the Iraq constitution develop in fear and trembling and have nothing to say about it. Iraq took about a year to reach a provisional agreement among three parties, but not four, on the basis of a draft provided by the greatest constitutional authorities in Washington. Then the voting was protected by 150,000 of the best armed soldiers in the world. It does not matter how sovereign you claim to be if there is no broadly based concensus that democracy is the only acceptable form of government. That means a willingness to accept whatever an electoral majority decides, confident that the opportunity may come to change it if the expected benefits are not achieved. Is that what the P.Q. will offer?

If not, the P.Q. should ask itself, and not the electorate of Quebec, whether it has any realistic prospect of success if it becomes separate from English speaking people.

And what will happen in Quebec and in Canada in the meantime? Far far better would be a new negotiation with Canada without pre-conditions, threats or unrealistic expectations.

Open Letter to Quebec City:

Sovereignty is a snare and a delusion
Creating disappointment and confusion;
All politics are local, so are yours
The Francophonie cannot open doors.

Please repeal your language legislation
And become the best bilingual nation;
Since 1760 we have been your friends
Let us return to discussing means and ends.

——◦ɤ◦——

DEMOCRACY

The British Constitution, like the language, developed by trial and error over many centuries, resolving one problem after another to the satisfaction of people who wanted freedom from tyranny. It was not a system of government imposed from above and is still unwritten. It is infinitely adjustable by a majority of representatives elected to a central parliament for a limited number of years. That was the first democratic process that anyone knows about and many people think it is still the best.

The two party system makes civil war unlikely. The majority party does not need to put the army to work while it has the civil power in its hands. The rest of the population does not resort to violence because they know they are in a minority. The politicians with a majority are willing to call an election every four years because they know a minority can be driven too far.

England had had plenty of experience with civil wars. Eventually, everyone wanted strong central government because they knew what life was like without it. Nasty, brutish and short.

When there are three parties, and nowadays the prospect of ten, the potential for strong government is less and may even be non-existent. As long as there is no incentive to resort to civil war that may not be such a bad thing. The American Constitution gives the impression that the founding fathers were trying to make strong government impossible unless the country is almost unanimous, or at the very least two thirds in favour of each matter of substance. In a federal state, and in a confederation such as Canada, there is something to be said in favour of delay, compromise and letting sleeping dogs lie. That was the policy of Horace Walpole, thought by some to be the finest English Prime Minister. He certainly governed democratically for 20 years of peace and prosperity.

With a few minor variations on this theme the English speaking countries are all democracies which relate back to the House of Commons in Westminster. That is also true for some of the countries which were prepared for self-government, however imperfectly, during their years of subservience as members of the British Empire. They will be democratic because they have fought against the alternatives so frequently and at such great cost. Democratic leaders prefer to fight another election than another war. These who have not yet lived in a democracy do not know what they are missing.

Some foreign governments call themselves democratic and even hold elections, not regularly but when they feel like it. English speaking people know when a country is democratic and when it is not. They do not have to prove it. That intuitive wisdom saves a lot of sophistry and unproductive argument. Tyranny is like pornography, we know it when we see it.

That is not to say that democracy provides the electorate with satisfactory government all of the time, or most of the time, or indeed any of the time. It is perfectly possible to live all of your life in a democracy and never have the party you voted for form a government; or if it does form a government, never to keep its election promises to your satisfaction. In addition, of course, you have the democratic freedom to change your own mind about parties, policies, economic decisions and foreign affairs whenever you want to. That may be the case in the middle of a term or in fact immediately following an election. People prefer to live in a democracy for one overriding reason: it saves them from having to fight in a civil war. As Winston Churchill was fond of saying, democracy is the worst form of government except for all the others.

And how did the community of nations respond to the television news and views from New York on 9/11?

Every country in the western world sent messages to Washington expressing a sense of shock, horror, and sympathy. The extent to which any of them offered to help the United States to rebuild is not known. No representatives flew to Washington to work out a common program of investigation, criminal law responsibility, border patrols or aircraft security in collaboration with USA. Nor in fact have any of them done so since.

Particularly shy of expressing opinions were the non-democracies but that was to be expected. Nor did any of them put their security into the hands of the United Nations. Nor did any of the democracies for that matter.

Some UN members knew of terrorist activities, training and planning within their own borders but no reports reached New York. The US posted rewards of many millions of dollars for information leading to the arrest of terrorists but there were no public trials. Every member of the UN appears to have taken the view that security was their business and no-one else's. Governments discussed the matter for a few days and released the comforting news to their own electorates that everything would be tightened up. Electorates answered opinion polls with their usual confidence based on complete ignorance of the nature of terrorist threats and the potential effect on the lives of all of us. Naturally they knew nothing about terrorism having only just heard of it. Without the slightest hesitation, for example, the Canadian public and the Federal Government confirmed that the five thousand mile undefended border would remain under their jurisdiction on the Canadian side. They would be glad to be left alone to deal with transit passengers and terrorists if any, thank you very much.

The thought that the United States Government might not be in complete agreement with that decision produced a reaction in Canada which can only be described as anti-American. When the US and a few allied forces tried to replace Saddam Hussein and hold elections there

was no support from Canada, rather the reverse. That was
not the democratic rejection of a close friend for sensible
reasons. It was national sovereignty with a vengeance.
It may be hoped that such short sighted foreign policies
will be reviewed in the light of the subsequent events
which demonstrated the incapacity of all nation states to
deal with global problems individually.

Some democracies are more intelligent than others
but they all appear to believe that no-one knows better
than themselves what is good for them. Delays in decision making are never caused by a determination to wait
for outside approval even amongst close friends. That is
a conditioned reflex resulting from centuries of nation-
state survival of the fittest which refers to the fitness to
survive in war. It is not a productive policy for the governments of small unarmed countries such as Canada
when asked to collaborate with the strongest military
power the world has ever seen.

Another thousand years of democracy may be required before national sovereignty can be discarded by
countries with widely divergent historical experiences
and whose highest priority is the survival of twenty five
separate languages. But among English speaking democracies it is perhaps time we all tried something new.

An excellent example could be set by Canada in the
matter of a small island in the Denmark Strait which is
claimed by both Canada and Denmark as sovereign territory. Statesmen can surely not covet even more oil than
Canada already has, especially oil which is two miles deep

in one of the roughest seas in the world. The Canadian Government should make a parcel of the legal deeds and present it to the Government of Denmark. Confirm that if ever they produce oil and deliver it to Canadian ports the provinces will be pleased to buy some of it at world prices.

—⚬—

CHAPTER TWELVE

IMMIGRATION

The poor huddled masses who emigrated to America in the eighteenth and nineteenth centuries were all running away from something. They left behind their country, their culture and in many cases their language. They were fed up, wherever they came from. They thought the melting pot was their salvation and they were happy to dive into it.

America needed people desperately and people arrived in their millions. Without immigration the United States would not have had young men and women to populate the West. But the American States did not have to advertise for immigrants or pay them to come. They would do anything to get there.

The first few years were always very hard. In some cases a new generation had to be born in America before they absorbed the language and the cultural climate. In the meantime they learned to read and write to some extent; they took every available job, sometimes two or three simultaneously; they got up early in the morning because they had to survive. They were never ashamed to perform personal services for the earlier arrivals who had started to get ahead. They were energetic, resourceful and ambitious people. After all, they were the ones who had the initiative to leave Europe when others stayed.

Immigrants were told that everyone is born equal but they did not believe it. They knew they were not equal at running the hundred-metre dash. All they thought the phrase meant is that they would have equal opportunity. There were limitations even to that pious hope but immigrants knew that in Europe they had had no opportunity at all. If you were not born into a good family and did not go to a good school you could never reach the higher levels of government or the professions. For one thing you could not speak properly. America was a dream world compared with that.

It is difficult to assess America if you have never lived there. Visitors from Europe jump to many false conclusions. Charles Dickens wrote a postscript for later editions of Martin Chuzzlewit that almost, but not quite, amounted to an apology for the scurrilous things he had said about immigrants.

> **"But what I have intended, what I have resolved upon is, on my return to England, in my own person, in my own Journal, to bear, for the behoof of my countrymen such testimony to the gigantic changes in this country as I have hinted at tonight".**

In other words, America had changed, not Charles Dickens. However it was enough. Thereafter Dickens was the most popular public speaker whenever he visited America.

Not all immigrants were successful of course. As in all human groups there were a minority with serious problems and a minority with above average intelligence and drive. The latter became the intellectual and financial leaders who set their own objectives and achieved them. But for everyone it was a competitive life and some degree of success came to all. If they needed to pick up sticks and move, they moved. To this day the mobility of labour in America is a significant economic advantage compared with the rigidity of European work forces.

Then came secondary waves of immigration from Europe as American families became able and willing to bring over friends and relations and help them to settle with them or near them. Again they came because they wanted to. No support was needed from government and none was offered. It may be supposed that the new immigrants were somewhat older and less adventurous than their American children. In some cases they were elderly parents who could not make much contribution to economic productivity. But everyone was welcome as long as America was thought to be a major improvement over life in Europe. Any slightest doubt on that subject was met by a stare of disapproval and the automatic question *"If you don't like it here, why don't you go back where you came from?"* Unanswerable.

As the standard of living increased and the demand for labour could not be met, new waves of immigrants arrived, legally or illegally, from Mexico and the Caribbean Islands. They were prepared to do work which was beneath the notice of existing Americans, even of the descendants of slaves. The new immigrants again came because they were wanted and they did in fact make an economic difference to the country. They also brought a new problem, which was a series of foreign languages that were difficult to absorb. The melting pot was still the ideal but it became impossible to insist on English schooling for all.

Communism in Cuba and some parts of South America produced refugees. In the twentieth century it became morally necessary for democratic states to provide a refuge for people who were denied freedom at home according to traditional standards. That introduced a completely new category of immigrants. They did not particularly want to move to America but they could not in all conscience be left where they were. They did not want to learn English so they might not integrate happily into the political and economic life of America but nowadays you cannot force people to speak your language if they do not want to. They had no families waiting to welcome them and help them to get started. What they really wanted was the American army to throw the communists out, in other words to reinstate the immigrants in their former circumstances. And that of course America proved unable to do.

One more problem arose in America, not directly the result of immigration but greatly complicating the melting pot philosophy. Religious fundamentalism makes it difficult to enforce the separation of church and state. It threatens the secular nature of education and the pre-eminence of the English language; and above all, it reduces the high degree of religious tolerance which had become normal in America. Deeply embedded in the North American folk memory was the appalling religious intolerance produced by the Reformation. Somehow, astonishingly, it was creeping back.

It does not seem a great deal to ask that every immigrant should be able to speak the language or be willing to learn it. That is not yet the approved policy of course but in most social situations America was setting a good example.

In these circumstances, the appearance of terrorism with a concentration of venom against the United States of America was an appalling shock to the self-confidence of all Americans. They are still wrestling with it.

Europe on the other hand had every reason to fear resentment from the people who had been left behind in their former colonies. It was generally believed, not always correctly, that the cult of empire had been based on economic enslavement; theft of valuable resources; imposed terms of trade; and destruction of local religions, cultures and languages.

The provision of infrastructure, schools, hospitals, investment capital and defence was not always adequate

but it certainly produced a political elite which was capable of providing self government in India, Pakistan,
Malaysia, and eventually in South Africa and in other
parts of the European colonial empires. But in other
places, especially in central and northern Africa, no such
claim can be made.

The most difficult situations arose where the colonial
governments were replaced by merciless dictators. No-
one could help the people of those states, not the UN,
not USA, not the IMF and certainly not the ex-colonial
powers. People had to be left to suffer in silence unless
they found a way to escape that is to say, become refugees, millions of them presently in camps in Africa on
the borders of unwilling hosts.

Here was a completely new category of immigrant.
People who felt aggrieved; robbed of their patrimony;
owed a living by persons unknown; and with no possible
alternative to immigration except torture, imprisonment,
starvation and death.

France had made every effort to prepare for such an
eventuality. The French colonies had become provinces
of France with representation in Paris, annual subsidies
and for all practical purposes, French citizenship. But
the numbers proved to be too great. The impossibility
of accepting all applicants and providing them with employment was regrettable to the French Government but
refusing entry gave the impression that France was admitting responsibility for the whole difficulty and was
unwilling to do anything about it. Terrorism arose in

France and elsewhere in the world because the disadvantaged people could see no other solution. Weapons and technology are readily available in the drug markets.

In varying degrees a threat to social stability will arise in all ex-colonial powers in Europe including England. Each country is studying its own particular challenge and trying to improvise counter-measures. There is no European co-ordination and in the absence of an agreed European constitution, none is likely to arise. The supremacy of the sovereign nation state is as strongly entrenched as ever and is making sure there will be no solution to immigration problems.

America has succeeded in absorbing immigrants to a total population of 350 million and has no immediate danger of civil war. Canada has done equally well in view of its bi-lingual constitution. Only in North America is there anything like experience, information and success on that scale. Yet European countries do not debate their immigration policies in Washington nor in the United Nations. They give a high priority to people who speak the same language, perhaps because they feel threatened worldwide by English speaking societies and economies.

Instead of spreading throughout each host country the immigrants settle in large language groups, which tend to cling to cultural and religious convictions that can prove unpopular locally. They encounter racism and discrimination. Employers are reluctant to risk alienating local people and the result is more unemployment not less. Then follow juvenile delinquency, demonstrations, riots and states of emergency. If the police lose control and the armed forces must be brought in it will be small consolation that the language has been saved.

Most unfortunate and incomprehensible. But the English speaking people are following down the same path. They should not encourage or permit the immigration of people who wish to preserve their own culture however incompatible it may be in their new country and who do not wish to earn their living using the English language. It is difficult for European countries to ignore threats to their languages but it is simply the case that the English language is not threatened anywhere. It does not seem too much to ask that every applicant should be willing to speak English at work and become culturally English or American as the case may be. They may speak their own language at home of course. In America the immigrants are well aware that they need to speak English as well as their original languages and usually do so.

However, America does not make it easy for immigrants to claim welfare benefits or subsidized housing. Whether legal or illegal they can get jobs easily but must make a substantial contribution to the economy before they can be accepted as American citizens. In Europe, on the other hand, the governments protect their labour markets but generally provide substantial welfare benefits from the date of arrival. It is clear which system is more conducive to globalization.

Political correctness has obscured these self-evident realities and somehow it must be replaced by logic. The English speaking electorates must create a balance in these matters.

CHAPTER THIRTEEN

———◦◦———

ECONOMICS

Economics professors report that students today are more interested in macroeconomic analysis than microeconomics, the theory of the firm. Young adults move directly from high school into the Stock Exchange, party politics and national budgets. But if government policies are not firmly grounded on microeconomic theory they are almost certain to result in disappointment. Regrettably, therefore, this chapter may read like an elementary text book but it provides the essential basis for all subsequent chapters.

The economic production and distribution of goods and services can only proceed on the basis of the rule of law. No one except in wartime will work to produce more than his own subsistence if any surplus would be seized by soldiers, the local lord of the manor or any totalitarian government, in other words, any group with the power of confiscation.

The specialization of labour, mass production and trade all depend on private ownership and the freedom to negotiate enforceable contracts beneficial to both parties. In a free enterprise economy an exchange will not take place if one or both parties think they may be dissatisfied with the result and certainly there would be no repeat business if either party regretted the transaction. Nor will it take place if one party believes the other can easily renege on agreements, written or verbal.

The economic activity of private business is sometimes thought of as dog eat dog but that could never be a stable basis of operation. Shop lifters and pirates and smugglers and renegade businessmen break the law and so, in many parts of the world can governments themselves, but in doing so they all reduce the social benefit which can be provided to society as a whole. In particular they reduce profit, which is the excess of benefits over costs, the basis of advancement of the entire economy.

A healthy economy can perhaps survive if the criminal underclass does not exceed approximately 10% of the population, including people who resent discipline, drug addicts or those who, for whatever reason, refuse to work or to cooperate with the authorities and who have to be paid for by everyone else. If the total becomes more than 10 in each hundred of the population, that society is in danger of collapse. It will become too costly to maintain as a democracy. And, without democracy, anything can happen.

If such a situation arises it cannot be corrected by moral persuasion or religious dogma. A country is either sufficiently law abiding or it is not. People who want to live in peace and comfort must be prepared to accept the costs of doing so.

When a country appears to be moving in the direction of anarchy it is not investment-worthy, whether it pretends to be democratic or not. And without investment there can be no creation of wealth.

The primary responsibility of honest government is to create conditions favourable to the development of a law-abiding society, and then to persuade everyone to accept it. The economic production and exchange of goods and services should then proceed freely and without government intervention for the most part. It is now becoming clear that everyone in the world is dependent on everyone else, and anyone who reduces total prosperity reduces it for themselves as well as everyone else.

Economics describing free enterprise is an English language science. Adam Smith wrote An Inquiry into the Nature and Causes of the Wealth of Nations and it was published in 1776, the same year as the American Declaration of Independence. Smith made the case that the baker does not supply you with bread because he likes you or because of any social obligation but because it is in his own personal interest to do so. Otherwise he would stop baking bread and do something else. And so for every other form of economic production in excess of the home requirements of the producer.

If governments reduce the freedom of individuals to manufacture and trade, they will reduce the total potential benefit to society and incidentally to the governments which tax them on a percentage basis. That is what Adam Smith was the first to point out.

It must be observed that he did not develop his economic theories out of his own imagination. He studied the history and current activities of man earning his living and came to the conclusion that, if governments abstained from interfering with free enterprise and free competition, industrial and commercial problems would work themselves out and the practical maximum efficiency would be reached. That same observation applied to international relations and is the classical argument in support of free trade. Smith did not say that this ought to happen as some sort of moral or ethical recommendation. He said that is what in fact does happen, and always did happen whenever wealth had been created, back to the trading empires of the Phoenicians, the Venetians and everyone else who had made money instead of losing it. All that was necessary to maximize the net benefit was for governments to get out of the way.

Nevertheless governments frequently did intervene in the market place and still do in many ways. The worst historical case was the English tariff on corn, which was designed to protect English farmers. They presumably became better off but at the cost of mass starvation in Ireland when the potato crops failed for several years running. Eventually the Prime Minister, Sir Robert Peel, crossed the floor of the House of Commons to vote with the opposition and repealed his own corn laws. A superb example to all future prime ministers in every country in Europe but an example rarely followed. The French government is still protecting 3% of its population at the expense of 97% of its consumers and of agricultural producers in the rest of the world.

The worst that can be said against Adam Smith in France is that his economic theory is self-evidently incorrect because it is Anglo-Saxon. It is a problem in all national politics to leave behind traditional views and rethink the decisions which resulted in unforeseen consequences. Good managers are not people who never make mistakes. They are people who recognize and correct their mistakes very rapidly. Governments are bad managers in the economic context, perhaps because their electorates punish them if they admit any possibility of having made a mistake. The fact remains that economic activity is self-correcting and government is not.

Karl Marx took the view that capitalism contained the seeds of its own destruction and was pre-destined to disappear. Instead of waiting for it to disappear the Marxist-Communist regime in Russia killed many millions of people including its own farmers to make sure that capitalism would disappear and in Russia it did for many years. But that did not make the Russian people as contented as those in America, nor as those in England and France for that matter, where they did not swallow the prescription quite so uncritically.

The Russian economy eventually collapsed and now there is no economic theory of any substance except Adam Smith. Yet governments still find it difficult to leave economic decisions to individuals in the market place. Governments should make macro-economic decisions on the evidence of market requirements but many countries have not thoroughly absorbed the lessons of the Russian experiment.

This is an even more important consideration in Europe than in the English speaking countries. Mercantilism in France, National Socialism in Germany, Italy and Spain, the temptations of Marxist Communism in all countries produced a mind-set which is incompatible with free enterprise. An uneasy compromise can be reached between the advantages of free trade and apparent national self-interest but globalization is not yet a popular concept. Economic theory in translation is not convincing to xenophobic electorates. Adam Smith must be read in the original English to make any sense.

The responsibility of governments to preserve law and order is not of course the only concern of the businessmen and their corporate policies. In the countries which have not yet adopted some form of democracy it is virtually impossible to generate profits and reinvest them in the companies which made them. Profits are redirected to armaments or the construction of palaces or the personal aggrandizement of dictators and politicians to an almost unlimited degree. No long term economic benefit can be expected in these circumstances. Only the full freedom of production and distribution by individual entrepreneurs can benefit society indefinitely into the future. Those who do not believe it will suffer economically as they have always suffered.

This does not mean there should be no taxation. The maintenance of infrastructure, defence and security and law and order is of course costly. Governments may also tax and spend in respect of information systems, health, welfare and education. If those sorts of benefits can be provided without adversely affecting the productivity of the economy then perhaps even more can be done centrally. But do not kill the geese which lay the golden eggs, as the British Government did when it nationalized all of their key industries in 1946. That is the extreme to be avoided. Having learned that lesson, where do we stand today?

In the time of Adam Smith the entrepreneur provided his own land, labour and capital, and his skill at designing and implementing his economic plan. That is to say, he combined the four factors of production to produce goods and services which were worth more in the open market than it had cost to produce them. If he did not make a profit he went out of business or started making something else. In these circumstances he paid all of the costs and retained all of the profit which was left over. There was no-one else to claim any of it.

Now all of the factors of production are separated among different people. Capital is supplied by investors, banks and financial markets. They demand a return, called interest or dividends at the market rate, otherwise they would not reinvest any more capital and nor would anyone else. But labour also must be rewarded with an acceptable return, otherwise the employees would leave and work somewhere else. And landlords must receive the accepted rent for the land and buildings they provide. And suppliers must be paid for their raw materials and semi-finished products. And the managers and directors of course would not perform the entrepreneurial functions if they were not paid the going rate. All factors of production must be paid enough to persuade them not to withdraw their services.

In this new world there is no point in calling private enterprise the capitalist system. Capital is essential but so are the other three factors of production, in varying proportions of course. And the owners of invested capital do not own the productive resources. A corporation is a legal person. If it acts to your detriment you must take it to court. You cannot sue the shareholders or banks or bondholders nor can you sue the employees. So what does ownership by shareholders mean? Very little. For all practical purposes we may suppose that corporations own themselves.

This argument has not yet been accepted by the public as a conclusive reason for avoiding the term capitalism but a better way of describing economic activity is free enterprise. It should not even be called the free enterprise system because no-one invented a system or enforces it or does anything but share in its revenue when it succeeds in operating at a profit. It is the organization which benefits from the surplus each year and it is that surplus which ensures its survival.

The more profit, the higher the wages and salaries may be negotiated; the better prices may be paid to landlords and suppliers; the higher the interest and dividends may be paid as the competitive market requires it; and the more taxes will be due to governments. To ensure that these revenues will continue, all of the factors of production must receive their expected rewards but a profit must continue to be earned at least to the same level as the closest competitors in the same type of business. The factors must all be mutually supportive or they will fly apart. It is the organization which keeps them together.

Business is not a zero-sum game. The creation of wealth can continue indefinitely if the excess revenue is reinvested properly. Otherwise, the business will fail sooner or later.

This description of present day economic reality is a serious denunciation of the industrial policy of many governments and to some extent of the Quebec and Canadian governments. That is another aspect of political life which the P.Q. will have to reassess to the satisfaction of the referendum electorate. Every country must adjust to the economic requirements of world markets and not to the pressure of groups of its own producers. The delusion of sovereignty will not inspire genius. It is more likely to warp the national judgement.

Among the many words of wisdom we receive from Dr. Johnson is the following: "*A man is seldom so innocently employed as when he is making money.*"

When a man is not busy he will get into trouble. That is not usually the case with the ladies, who are busy all of their lives with their children and their own requirements. But the best cure for all forms of problem, mental and physical, is to keep busy.

Business, of course, derives from busy-ness.

———∽———

CHAPTER FOURTEEN

RATES OF INTEREST

There is something very wrong with the present-day concept of interest rates and their supposed connection with the Bank Rate in each country. The world has changed but our theory has not changed with it. A complete re-think is required.

It is the responsibility of commercial banks, mortgage institutions, retail stores and credit card companies to charge rates of interest which cover the risk of loss in each case. It is clear that this is a matter for private enterprise and that the correct "rate of interest" in each case will be decided in competitive markets. Those who lend at the correct rate will remain profitable and those who do not will go bankrupt.

Similarly with loans to entrepreneurs and individuals for business development purposes. The interest rates will tend to equate the supply and demand for investment capital and reward the lending organizations which most correctly evaluate the risk in each case. No-one would argue that all business loans should be made at the same rate of interest.

Similarly for bonds and shares offered on the stock exchanges; each purchaser makes his own evaluation of the risk and buys or sells accordingly. Those decisions result in a single market price for each asset which is the same for all buyers and sellers but it varies from day to day and minute to minute.

And similarly for insurance companies. Actuaries do not pretend that their projections are scientifically accurate. Premiums must be re-assessed continuously and adjusted in the light of experience and changing demand for each type of coverage. The insurers must stay in business in order to pay the claims and to do that they must remain profitable, no matter how high the claims may prove to be. It would be impossible for all insurers to offer insurance at rates set by their governments.

When governments claim to be "the insurer of last resort" they mean that they will if necessary pay claims out of the public purse. In other words, many people would contribute without themselves having been covered by the insurance. Such involvement of government in the private sector was perhaps unavoidable in sovereign states which had to rely on their own resources but the global supply and demand potentials today make that unnecessary. And fortunately so, now that all countries face global warming or cooling, terrorism, violent governments, religious fervour and a general increase in unpredictability. Only world wide collaboration can deal with these situations.

A Bank Rate is the rate of interest charged by each central bank for money supplied to the commercial banks in unlimited quantities on an overnight basis. The charge could be zero, as it was for six years in Japan. In 2006 the Japanese Government raised its Bank Rate to 0.25% and that was considered by financial observers to indicate a dramatic change of policy. However, a bank rate of 0.0% or 0.25% can have no possible connection to the calculation of interest rates charged by private enterprise. But still it is believed by all authorities that Japan was an odd exception. Everyone else in the world is believed to be bound by the local Bank Rate when assessing the risk premiums they must charge.

There is no reason for central banks to raise additional tax revenue when providing the fiduciary issue which it is their responsibility to do. It is not supposed that the Bank Rate covers any risk that the commercial banks may default. To make a profit is a time honoured custom within each country which has no relation to the demand for world capital. Certainly it has no relation to the rates of interest charged by commercial institutions which naturally vary in each country. Lenders must take into account the demand for capital and for insurance coverage, the climate, political and economic stability, recent history and the skill of actuaries, accountants and business managers. None of these factors is affected by alterations in the Bank Rate.

But governments pretend that they are. If all interest rates including the Bank Rate were set by internal supply and demand conditions, there would be nothing for each central bank to do, except to print the notes and mint the coins. Governments theoretically set the central

banks free to supply the currency when it is needed and
control the economic environment but in practice they
never remove themselves far from the scene of decision
making.

The central banks claim that they are "fighting inflation" but that raises another entire spectrum of misunderstandings. To provide social services without
proportionate taxation, the post-war governments in
Europe and elsewhere indulged in massive deficit spending. They apparently believed they were taking the advice of the greatest economist of the twentieth century
but they were not.

John Maynard Keynes proposed that governments
should decrease taxes and spend their way out of a re-
cession on the downward turn of each trade cycle and
increase taxes again on the next upswing. He believed it
would be possible to balance the national budget over a
four or five year period and insisted that it was essential
to do so. The first part of the recommendation was eagerly adopted but the second part was ignored by almost all
governments until the interest rate for additional investment capital exceeded 20% per year. That finally raised
the spectre of the hyper-inflation which German people
inflicted on themselves between the wars.

Now that most governments finance their deficits
(if any) by borrowing rather than by printing additional
notes, there is no longer any inflation in the Keynesian
sense. But some consumer prices rise disproportionately
and the central bankers believe they are responsible for

holding "core inflation" to a maximum of 2% per year. When that number is exceeded (according to highly unreliable statistics) they increase the limit to 3% or whatever appears to be within their ability to control. If it exceeds 3% they blame someone else.

So governments are not in fact adjusting the Bank Rate to preserve interest rates at the correct levels, if in fact they ever did. They are making one quarter per cent changes to the Bank Rate in the vague hope that it will keep prices down, or some prices, or enough prices to keep the electorate happy. But a properly run country will be prosperous whatever the Bank Rate may be, providing it has no relation to the commercially viable interest rates in each country.

In North America there is a widespread belief that the best measure of a currency's true value is its price in gold. The Fed is advised by eminent authorities to use gold as its guide in its fight against inflation, and leave short term interest rates alone. Unfortunately, there is not a word of truth in that theory. The price of gold fluctuates far more than the rate of inflation and frequently in the opposite direction. The price of gold would drop practically to zero if the experts in Washington decided to finance imports by selling some or all of the gold in Fort Knox, which one of these days they may very well have to do. What would be the effect of that on the rate of inflation in each country? We do not know.

Stable exchange rates and the purchasing power within each country are the result of economic performance, country wide and globally. If rates of interest are inappropriate they should be permitted to move freely, without let or hindrance by any government, and with no concern about the price of gold.

The present unsatisfactory state of affairs is complicated by the modern attitude to personal debt. Consumers in the 21st Century are choosing to maintain all expenditures and go into debt rather than economise. For example, when the cost of gasoline increases, drivers tend to travel the same distances. That would not matter if they reduced their expenditures on other goods and services but they choose to maintain and even increase all of their expenditures. They go into debt for long periods of time when they should be saving for their old age.

People borrow by using credit cards and not paying them off at the end of each month, even though compound interest accumulates at rates exceeding 20% per year. In addition people sign mortgages and they buy cars and durable consumer goods over 5 years on terms which may prove to be beyond their capacity to fulfil. That seems to be too little money chasing too many goods, which should eventually cause disinflation, but in the meantime, more and more people are living beyond their means and do not seem to be worrying about it.

Personal indebtedness in North America may now be as great in total as government indebtedness became through uncontrolled deficit spending. Even that may not result in disaster as long as the lending institutions survive and if the governments do not take to the printing press again. It is the lack of transparency, the lack of correct analysis and the obsession with national sovereignty which create the problems.

When the government reduces taxes, consumers may be pleased to spend the money themselves instead of trusting the government to distribute it wisely, even if it adds to inflationary pressure. A majority of people may even vote for it. But inflation at present levels may no longer deserve such a bad name. The velocity of circulation always increases on the upswing of each trade cycle but not by much, especially as expenditure is now not only in liquid currency. Credit cards, bank payments and computer transactions are all the result of individual decision making. Governments could ask, if they wish, to be absolved of responsibility for containing inflation. Individuals as well as corporations can get into trouble but no amount of government intervention could save them all. Let us resurrect buyer beware and learning from experience in this new global economy.

World wide, we now need to concentrate on microeconomic analysis; the theory of the firm and individual consumer behaviour. Macro-economic theory developed by economists employed by governments will invariably be used to justify intervention in the market place. Now is the time to evaluate the costs and benefits over the last twenty years of macro-economic model building and investigate alternative policies. Globalization based on individual choices is more likely to succeed than world government or any approximation to it. Above all, we do not want, and we do not need, anything which could be described as a global rate of interest.

CHAPTER FIFTEEN

———✧———

OIL

The production and distribution of oil is the best example we have of globalization. Other industries can learn from the history of the oil business and the futile efforts of all governments to control it.

Before OPEC, world oil exploration and development were virtually controlled by seven companies known as The Seven Sisters. The managers knew each other, and as Adam Smith had predicted, they seldom met together even for diversion and merriment without it resulting in a conspiracy against the public. So the public thought. It was in fact a cartel opproximating quite closely to a world-wide monopoly. It set the price of a barrel of oil at the level customers were prepared to pay for the total quantity of oil the companies were producing. That was a quantity which increased every year after America began the mass production of cars and when the American public became able to buy those cars. As Europe and other parts of the world became wealthy enough to buy cars, of course the demand for oil increased proportionately. There was no better means of individual transportation and no technology as efficient as the internal combustion engine. Nor is there to this day.

Oil bubbled out of the ground to some extent but the increasing demand could only be met by drilling deep into the earth and pumping oil to the surface. That involved problems of drilling, collection, flow control, filling containers, transportation world-wide, storage and dealing with fire hazards.

The technology to solve all of those problems was developed by American engineers and later spread to other countries where oil was discovered, mainly in the Middle East. England, France and other European countries found oil in some of their colonies and developed the industry on behalf of their subjugated peoples.

America did not have any empire to speak of and the US companies had to negotiate with local governments wherever they found oil. In effect, they rented the oil fields. It was not difficult to obtain concessions on mutually agreeable terms because none of the governments in the Middle East were democracies. The local authorities had absolute sovereignty according to the criteria of the League of Nations and later of UNO. Unfortunately for their own population almost all of their share of the oil revenues was spent on their own royal families, sheiks and religious leaders. Very little of it was reinvested in the oil industry and the Seven Sisters continued to do all of the work, training, marketing and exploration. They were well paid and so were the governments but ordinary people were hardly any better off than they had been before oil was discovered. The only means of transportation in their own countries continued to be the camel which saved the expense of building roads across the deserts.

During the reign of the Seven Sisters you could drive a car, if you had one, anywhere in the world. In every town and village a private enterprise distributor was selling gasoline at a price the car and truck drivers could afford. You could buy any make of tires, batteries, fan belts and other spare parts, and have your mechanical problems corrected reasonably quickly. Nobody held you up for ransom. It would have been absurd for the Seven Sisters to set prices for oil or gasoline which would have stopped people from driving. Naturally prices go up as exploration and distribution costs increase but the increase in supply will only occur if the demand increases to take all of the extra oil at whatever the world price of oil happens to be. That is the natural result of globalization.

Many people and their governments believe that the use of cars should be restricted because they cause air pollution. To be consistent they should welcome higher prices for gasoline every year to encourage research to replace the internal combustion engine. In fact they could look forward happily to the time when there will be no more oil. But they do not. On this subject, as on many others, electorates and governments are ambivalent to an extreme degree.

From the point of view of the public there is not much to fear from cartels, anti-trust legislation or no anti-trust legislation. Cartels draw attention to profit margins which justify further investments by the cartel or by new entries to the industry. They also greatly benefit the communities which impose profit taxes.

According to governments, profit is a good thing in some circumstances and a bad thing in others. They are obviously defining profit in different ways at different times, if in fact they ever attempt to define profit at all.

The Seven Sisters were unchallenged for a long time because other countries did not have the necessary know-how or experienced personnel. It was an English language industry and still is to a large extent. After WWII the European expatriates withdrew from their colonial territories and were replaced by local staff, frequently recruited and trained by English speaking technicians. The revenue was collected and spent in local currencies and by civil servants speaking local languages but the technology and world marketing expertise was available everywhere in English. The local ownership did not make much difference to the fact that the operation of the world industry was still the responsibility of the Seven Sisters and a few new multi-national corporations which carried on doing exactly what they had been doing before.

OPEC is a loose association of countries which took over oil wells from America and the Europeans. OPEC members benefit greatly from the increasing demand for oil but they are not concerned with the cost of refining or distributing the products derived from oil. They charge as much as they can for the oil as it comes out of the ground, and their prices are higher than the prices which used to be charged by the Seven Sisters. There is no evidence that any of the members of OPEC reduced production in order to increase the price per barrel of oil in their own countries. They would be foolish to do so because the demand for oil is highly inelastic. A lower selling price would be certain to reduce total revenue and it would hardly increase the quantity sold at all.

Equally, there is no evidence that any of the OPEC countries could increase production at short notice. They all pump everything they can all of the time. Additional quantities could only be produced on the basis of additional investment capital and more outside expertise. It is in the interest of every producer to sell at the highest price available and they all do.

Increasing production requires oil to be pumped greater distances and from greater depths. Why would any country invest additional capital if the objective would be to reduce the price of oil? That would automatically result in a negative rate of return on capital taken directly from the pockets of the owners. None of them are as stupid as that.

Claims by OPEC that they produce 25% of the world's oil and are therefore in a position to control the world price may be totally discounted. It is smoke and mirrors.

The world price of oil is increasing because the demand for cars in China, India and elsewhere is increasing much faster than the supply of oil is increasing. It has nothing to do with the deliberations of OPEC one way or the other.

Now suppose that western governments wish to intervene in the market place, not to maximize profits but to drive prices down. That would tend to increase the effective demand and the problem of pollution, at the cost of heavy subsidies contributed by other tax payers. To solve those problems the governments would have to permit the price of oil to rise, which is what the Seven Sisters always did, to the point where supply equals demand. It is not clear why any government wishes to intervene in that process but from time to time they all do.

Simultaneously with their attempts to reduce the profitability of the oil companies, governments tax the use of oil heavily which increases the cost of driving. That can be a rational policy if the revenue is used to solve the problems of poverty, crime, health and welfare, and so on. Unfortunately there is not much pressure on governments to do that. Money is just as frequently wasted as used productively, especially when it is easily come by.

A country which contains large deposits of oil, gas, gold or diamonds is in a position to attract investors who will provide the governments with a large revenue every year, whether or not they contribute any capital themselves. No-one can interfere with the right of governments to do anything they like with the money they receive and certainly the United Nations Organization will not.

That is why all governments are dedicated to the principle of national sovereignty. To them it means freedom not for the electorates but for themselves. It is necessary to face the fact that nothing can be done to distribute oil revenues more widely until autocratic governments are replaced by democratic assemblies, and even then there is no agreement about what governments should do and what they should not do.

It was assumed until recently that in the Middle East the poor people would enthusiastically welcome democracy if ever they were offered that opportunity. Our experience in oil producing countries in this century indicates that the world may not be that simple. We must keep trying to influence other countries by a good example but it may take a long time.

Why does the price of oil fluctuate so much if it is simply a function of existing supply and continuously growing demand? It is because each point in the delivery chain has a limited storage capacity. At the refinery level, purchasing agents can only bring in oil to the extent that demand can be estimated for each grade of gasoline, aviation fuel, petrochemical stock, heating oil and residual products. As temporary shortages arise, supplies must be brought in at almost any price. When oil futures have been paid for and prove to be more than needed, no orders will be placed for future delivery and the market price may drop steeply. Nevertheless it is the long-term supply and demand relationship which counts. Short-term forecasts may all be ignored by the investing public.

A growing middle class in China is said to be approximately 30% of the population. Within a few years that could become equal to the entire population of the United States. What will the demand for oil become if every Chinese family in that 30% can afford to buy a car? And why should they not? We all did.

Then there is India, potentially even greater numbers, to say nothing of South East Asia and South America. We will be fortunate if we can develop new sources of energy to keep pace with that, but one thing we know, we cannot stop them driving cars.

In these circumstances the production and distribution of oil is totally beyond the control of national governments, however sovereign they may all pretend to be. Research into improved engines, less pollution and new forms of applied energy becomes a worldwide challenge. And so it will be for all industries which become globalized. That is not a threat to international stability. It is the only possible solution to our problems.

As Shakespeare predicted in Macbeth, we will all
benefit.

> **The weird sisters, hand in hand**
> **Posters of the sea and land**
> **Thus do go about, about;**
>
> **Double, double, toil and trouble**
> **Oil-well burn, refinery bubble;**
>
> **Fair is foul and foul is fair**
> **Hover through the fog and filthy air.**
>
> **O! Well done! I commend your pains**
> **And every one shall share i' the gains.**

CHAPTER SIXTEEN

———ঞ্চ———

TERRORISM

The human senses are fallible. People who share a common experience can remember it differently, especially after a long period of time. They can interpret it differently, that is to say, learn different things from it. Seeing is believing for almost everyone, but eye witnesses frequently contradict each other. That is where scientific method comes in.

There are five stages to every scientific investigation:

1. A question must be clearly expressed concerning an apparent cause/effect relationship, a controversy between two scientists or a prediction, which is important enough to justify more research.

2. Possible explanations are considered and for each one a hypothesis is invented based on general scientific theory and a comprehensive set of assumptions, which must be stated in writing.

3. For each hypothesis the history of the subject must be reviewed, all relevant data collected and all previous experi-

ence and observations discussed among
equals.
4. The hypothesis which seems most likely
to be true is then selected, preferably the
most simple of all possible explanations.
Here we are dealing with probability
theory. In science there is no certainty.
5. The selected hypothesis is checked by a
series of observations, experiments and
further discussion, particularly with opponents of that hypothesis. The hypothesis may be accepted as a valid theory
when there is no disagreement among
scientists.

Every hypothesis and every scientific theory is thrown
into doubt and temporarily discarded when any observation anywhere in the world appears to provide an exception to it or to require additional experimental evidence.
If there is one single exception to the hypothesis it must
be discarded. In science the exception does not prove the
rule, it replaces it.

If one person holds a religious belief which directly
contradicts the belief of another, they cannot both be
right. Most probably they are both wrong, at least to
some extent. But human beings find it difficult to accept
that there is any possibility they may be wrong, especially in religious matters. There is a universal craving
for certainty. Religious people use the word 'believe' to

mean absolute certainty. That is why they are all un-scientific.

When non-religious people use the word 'believe' they mean that to the best of their knowledge it is so. They only think their statements are correct, especially if they refer to future expectations. They have no problem when other people disagree. They simply decide whether to change their minds or not.

Some of the most unpleasant behaviour in history occurred during the Reformation and Counter Reformation in the sixteenth century. People picked sides as to whether they would be Catholic or Protestant. There was nothing in between. We have to admit that the English speaking people were no better than anyone else. When face to face with each other, and in a position of temporary superiority, they used torture, burning at the stake, damning to all eternity and international war to prove their point. It is not easy today to establish exactly what their differences of opinion were but they all became terrorists when their beliefs were contradicted.

Finally after many years of cruelty to each other, the people of Europe discovered a common sense solution. It was called religious tolerance. I will let you believe anything you want to believe if you will let me believe anything I want to believe. Live and let live. I will continue to believe that I am right and you are wrong but we will stop talking about it. That permitted the Enlightenment to proceed on a scientific basis, the industrial revolution to work its miracles in England, and the Empire to be established in territories inhabited by people with completely alien cultures without wanting to kill them all. The differences of opinion persisted but economic competition replaced personal hatred.

The development of the nation-state system with unquestioning tribal loyalty and the acceptance of war as a instrument of national policy had many of the attributes of religious faith and so, later, did Marxist-Communism, but it was becoming easier to see through the façade. In the twentieth century, most people decided they did not want to go to war against their fellow human beings if they could possibly avoid it. In the implementation of this resolve, unfortunately, they failed their fellow human beings miserably.

We imagined in our innocence that everyone had entered the twenty-first century in approximately the same frame of mind. Now we know that in the Middle East it was not so. We could not understand our next-door neighbours in England in the Reformation so it is not likely that discussions in Arabic will resolve our disagreements with Muslims. We may all believe something because we were told it when we were children. It is not unscientific because it is wrong. It may well be right. But it is unscientific because it has not passed through the five stages. It is an unsubstantiated hypothesis and that is all.

The American invaders of Iraq expected to be welcomed with joy and gratitude as Holland greeted our troops in 1944. Most of the Iraqi people had suffered as much as the Dutch and probably even more. Liberation and democratic elections were certain to be universally popular, we thought. Now we know that a civil war could only be avoided by a long term occupation and suicide bombing would become a standard method of dissent as long as infidels remained on their soil.

Perhaps when the foreign armies are absent the seeds of democracy will flourish but that is by no means certain. What the Arab countries have never had, and what they desperately need, is a native Francis Bacon to tell them what science is, and what it is not.

In the meantime it is clear that the English speaking people cannot march from country to country bringing with them the eagerly awaited benefits of western civilization. People must work out their future for themselves, however long it may take. We can only hope that religious fanaticism and terrorism will soon be a small percentage of each population. Perhaps we can handle that.

Trade will continue to provide economic benefits in every part of the world as it has always done. That can be left to the entrepreneurs to organize. Governments cannot assess the risks very well but individual traders always do, language and legal problems notwithstanding. We do not need armies to identify economic opportunities. And what can armies do in the Middle East? Not very much apparently.

Cooperation with friendly nations in the development of resources, communications and the control of terrorists and religious fanaticism is desirable and feasible, with the prior agreement that a legitimate government requests our presence. Otherwise the overriding principle is perhaps to live and let live by staying away, as long as they are willing to live in peace.

There are four social characteristics, which constitute warning signals against any close relationships with a foreign country:

1. Terrorism, which the government cannot or does not want to control.
2. Theocracy.
3. Belief in the occupation of territory by infidels.
4. Official opposition to democracy and widespread denial of human rights particularly for women.

Countries exhibiting these unpleasant symptoms will slowly but surely self-correct but it may take a long time. We cannot help by being physically present.

We should provide free television and education in the use of scientific method. We should shine the searchlight of world opinion on every piece of evidence we can find, which demonstrates how illogical their behaviour is. And that we can do at a distance if only we can find out what is happening.

Concerning the philosophy of potential terrorists we may consider the story, perhaps apocryphal, about an Imam who blew himself up with the explosives he had permitted the faithful to store in his Mosque. He may not have expected to receive the same fringe benefits he had promised to genuine suicide bombers but he would surely not have feared that he would be refused entry to Paradise altogether. All true believers are certain they are on the side of the angels, even when they are incompetent failures.

Crusaders were undoubtedly the same in their day. Christianity has been practised for a much longer time than Islam and may have resulted in many more disappointments than triumphal entries into Heaven. But no-one ever thought that acceptance of their religious faith would reduce their chances of resurrection. No-one has had any previous experience in these matters.

Religious conviction cannot be disputed because there is no possibility of finding evidence that it may be incorrect. We cannot win an argument with a suicide bomber because he is not listening. Diplomacy cannot resolve that problem or even define it. Present day political correctness forbids us even to discuss such questions. The only hope we have of peaceful co-existence with religious extremists is that they will stop believing in an after-life altogether. There is no place for compromise with terrorists on this subject or any other.

The best illustration of these difficulties is present day Lebanon.

———⌥———

CHAPTER SEVENTEEN

LEBANON

Lebanon, at the eastern end of the Mediterranean, was the home of the Phoenicians. The greatest explorers and traders of the ancient world. Their ships connected the caravans on the Silk Road from China to the tin mines of Cornwall and all major ports in between. Such a history might reasonably have made Lebanon a role model for the global economy. It seems to have been the development of nation states which prevented free trade from unifying the world under the leadership of the Phoenicians.

As in many other countries, Lebanon remained a trading nation but suffered from civil wars, extreme differences of religious beliefs, massacres, and interference by foreign powers. For several centuries the entire area was occupied and controlled by the Ottoman Turks. That is how so many people became Muslims, whether they were Arabs or not. In the case of Iran, the people were not Arabs at all. They had descended from the Persians, another mighty empire in their time.

Palestine and Lebanon became geographical terms under the Ottoman Empire and not countries at all, in the United Nations sense. They all had mixed populations of Arabs, Muslims, Jews, Christians and others.

During WWI the British army defeated the Turks in the Middle East and took control of Palestine. France took control of Syria and Lebanon. The League of Nations confirmed many such occupations as Mandates, and left the Great Powers to govern as they wished.

After WWII, Britain accepted a UN vote to partition Palestine into two states, Israel and Palestine. After the 1948 war, Israel became independent and Palestine merged with Jordan. It is therefore incorrect to pretend that Israel was formed by invading other countries and seizing their land.

These facts are constantly denied by claiming that the land had been a gift provided by God. But that only made the diplomatic problem insoluble, because all parties made the same claim and presumably referred to the same God.

Syria tried to absorb Lebanon and assist Palestine to make war with Israel. At one point America and France tried to help Lebanon, but withdrew after 241 American service men and 58 French paratroopers were killed by Hezbollah suicide bombers in 1983.

After Israel had occupied South Lebanon for twenty-two years the soldiers of Israel and Syria withdrew and Lebanon was left to settle its own affairs. Investment capital flooded in and Lebanon was in the process of becoming a prosperous modern state. Beirut which had been considered the Paris of the Middle East, was once again living at peace with itself.

Elections were held and Lebanon formed a popular government but it could not control the militia in the South of Lebanon which continued to be supported by Syria and Iran. The military leadership of Hezbollah (The Party of God) based itself in Syria. The UN frequently demanded Hezbollah's disarmament, but the Lebanese Government said its army was too weak to oppose the guerrilla group.

UN Resolution 1559 required Lebanon to disarm Hezbollah. The Lebanese Government should have reported to the United Nations that they could not control events in their own territory but they did not. They continued in office hoping for the best and soon, of course, achieving the worst. If the electorate did not want Hezbollah to attack Israel they should not have voted for a government which included thirty-five members of Hezbollah. In a democracy the electorate must always blame itself when things go wrong, especially when disaster was clearly foreseeable. Hezbollah dug underground bunkers two and three stories deep and imported some 15,000 rockets from Iran via Syria. These preparations for war along the Israeli border took several years to complete, but the Lebanese Government did not request assistance from UNO and the UN did not offer any. In 2006 Hezbollah commenced a rocket barrage into Israel with the full knowledge of Iran and Syria and without expecting support from anyone else. The 1,990 UN "peace monitors" in South Lebanon since 1978 watched all of these proceedings without raising an alarm.

Israel attacked and invaded Lebanon because Hezbollah was firing rockets into its cities. No member of the United Nations would fail to respond to rocket attacks on its citizens, or to neighbours tunnelling under their borders. The UN would not expect them to. Nothing is more sacred to a nation than its territorial integrity. Whether the decision to attack Israel was made by Hezbollah, Syria or Iran made no difference to the fact that it was intended to produce a war against Israel on two fronts. No-one could have expected anything else. It was probably judged that America was too heavily involved in Iraq to be able to respond and that UNO would enforce a cease-fire to the benefit of Hezbollah.

Such long-term Machiavellian plans can only confirm the fact that some governments are determined to destroy Israel. Official statements have been made to that effect and now there is no reason to disbelieve them. Many people find it impossible to imagine that anyone could seriously propose a second holocaust, and almost everyone will find it difficult to believe. But that does appear to be the case, certainly for the Hezbollah.

In August 2006 the UN Security Council drafted a ceasefire agreement and presented it to Israel and the Lebanese Government. An agreement is something which has to be agreed. It cannot be imposed. Soldiers wearing blue helmets may help keep the peace but they cannot impose peace. It is Hezbollah which must sign a peace treaty but the Lebanese Government accepted the UN offer without even consulting Hezbollah. They knew what the answer would be. A properly negotiated peace would be the death of Hezbollah and their military leaders. That has nothing to do with disagreements among the fifteen members of the Security Council. The United Nations is not constituted to force a ceasefire on unwilling combatants. It is surprising that anyone ever thought it could, and after Rwanda, amazing.

On 12 August 2006, the Secretary-General of the United Nations announced that the fighting between Israel and Hezbollah would come to an end on 14 August at 0500 hours GMT. Israeli troops would withdraw from South Lebanon and be replaced by 15,000 men of the Lebanese army and 15,000 blue helmets under the leadership of France.

It was clear that Israel was not forced to accept this ceasefire by the United Nations but by the United States.

An Armistice was signed by both sides in 1918 and the First World War came to an end. But the German people knew that the Armistice was in fact a total surrender. Germany had no control over the terms of the Treaty of Versailles. And that would be the position of the Israeli Government if it agreed to a ceasefire which left Hezbollah still armed and belligerent. No country can surrender to governments which are dedicated to the removal of all infidels from their sacred soil. That would be asking Israel to accept the gas ovens again or be driven into the sea.

So the good people of Lebanon and in the rest of the world must wait patiently for sanity to return; also the peace loving people in Iraq, Sri Lanka, Africa, Kashmir, and everywhere else where violence breaks out. It is no use asking whose fault it is. The only final solution is democratic globalization and that may take many years to evolve.

But every cloud has a silver lining. There can now be no cause for concern that the Western Nations are the enemy of Islam because Islam as a whole does not want to destroy Israel.

The Indonesian Government, the largest Muslim country, does not want to destroy Israel. It is too busy keeping its own country together and preparing for the next tsunami. The first paragraph of the Indonesian Pancasila is "There is one God". They do not give him a name.

The Islamic tribes in Africa do not want to destroy Israel. They are hardly aware that Israel exists. They are fighting each other.

Egypt does not want to destroy Israel. The main threat to the stability of Egypt is its own religious extremists. Similarly in Algeria.

Pakistan does not want to destroy Israel. It would rather win the battle against India in the matter of Kashmir.

And Turkey? Kemal Ataturk shaved and wore a trilby hat in 1923.

The Muslims in North America do not want to destroy Israel. They want to preserve themselves and if possible everyone else under their banner. Israel is no threat to anyone.

Even the unpleasant young men in France who burn cars every night do not want to destroy Israel. They are totally self-absorbed with their own complaints and un-employment. They will get into trouble until they be-come busy. They are not potential suicide bombers in far away countries.

Who knows what North Korea wants? Nothing, in-cluding the destruction of Israel, would make North Korea happy.

In fact, the number of people actively working for the destruction of Israel is probably quite small. The young people in Iran are similar to the young people in Beirut in many ways, well educated, secular in many cases, anx-ious to get on with their own lives in peace. The problem is not the Islamic people, it is the theocracies which gov-ern them.

A theocracy cannot easily change its mind. If the President of Iran appeared on television and announced a new policy which recognized the right of Israel to exist, he would rapidly be replaced. Dealing with the present government of Iran and Syria will be very difficult; but it will be much easier than fighting against one billion people. We must count our blessings.

It should also be noted that the Shia and Sunni sects of Islam are not divided by religious differences. They disagree about the descent of their present religious lead-ers in a direct line from the Prophet. Christianity had

similar problems in the Middle Ages concerning its connection with St. Peter. Several Popes ruled Christendom
from Avignon in France, leaving the deposed Popes to
move for safety from Rome to the hill towns of Tuscany.
That is another reminder of the common factors in religious history. Perhaps we can create some fellow feelings on that basis.

Nation states do not develop into democracies until each population becomes an electorate which forces
kings, emperors, popes, imams and tribal war-lords to
surrender their powers to a popular assembly. That is the
surrender we are looking for. Governments never sur-
rendered their powers willingly in England, so they will
never give up anywhere unless they are forced to do so.

The main weapon in the past was to withhold taxes.
Without money the Emperor has no clothes. But that
weapon is not available for use against the governments
of Arab-Muslim countries which receive and retain the
revenues from oil production. There may be no other
way than the use of military force. The 300,000 people
who live in Lebanon must first demonstrate support of
their elected Government and renounce any desire they
may have had to destroy Israel. Then perhaps they can
live in peace without the danger of another war initiated
by Hezbollah. Then we can see what Iran and Syria will
do without them.

Terrorism will continue elsewhere no doubt but if we
resolve the Arab-Israeli conflict we will have the time

and energy to unite our global forces in support of civilization.

The English Speaking People must remove all possibility of a second holocaust as they eventually stopped
the first. Then they must rebuild Lebanon as they rebuilt
Germany and Japan. The Marshall Plan will become the
Bush Plan, or perhaps by then it will be the Mrs. Clinton
Plan. It will be expensive but not more expensive than
another holocaust.

—— ⚬⁄⚬ ——

CHAPTER EIGHTEEN

FREE WILL AND DETERMINISM

In your head are many vaguely held beliefs and disbe-
liefs and a few firmly based convictions. They do not
command universal acceptance, partly because there
are no words which accurately describe them and partly
because they contradict each other. Do not attempt to
elucidate them all. That would greatly increase the difficulty of loving your neighbour as yourself. But there
is one particular matter which has always caused more
difficulty than anything else and which is comparatively
simple to resolve – given of course some approximation
to an open mind. Are all of your actions predetermined?
Or can you exercise free will to some extent, in some
circumstances and at least occasionally?

In the Canterbury Tales, Geoffrey Chaucer summarized the controversy very well. That was in the four-
teenth century and the subject was already well known
and constantly debated. Here are the relevant lines from
the Nun's Priest's Tale, as translated into modern English
by Nevill Coghill and put back into the verse form used
by Chaucer (Penguin Books Limited, London (1986):

But that which God's foreknowledge can foresee
Must needs occur, as certain men of learning

Have said. Ask any scholar of discerning;
He'll say the Schools are filled with altercation
On this vexed matter of predestination
Long bandied by a hundred thousand men.
How can I sift it to the bottom then?
The Holy Doctor St. Augustine shines
In this, and there is Bishop Bradwardine's
Authority, Boethius' too, decreeing
Whether the fact of God's divine foreseeing
Constrains me to perform a certain act
- And by 'constraint' I mean the simple fact
Of mere compulsion by necessity –
Or whether a free choice is granted me
To do a given act or not to do it
Though, ere it was accomplished, God foreknew it,
Or whether Providence is not so stringent
And merely makes necessity contingent.

And those are still the unanswered questions for Christians, Jews and Muslims to this day. Were all improvements predetermined? Or can free will take some of the credit? Am I disappointed or pleased with my experience in time? And, what is time, anyway?

Perhaps the past is the past and the future is the future, the dividing line between them being the present. What prevents us from coming to that common sense conclusion? Only the controversy about free will and determinism.

Whenever a change occurs there is a situation before the change and a situation after the change. The situation which will exist after the change is the future, from the standpoint of the situation before the change. And the situation before the change is the past from the standpoint of the situation after the change.

But we have to accept that there is no common factor unifying those two standpoints. Looking forward in time is not at all the same thing as looking backward in time, only in a different direction. To clarify this statement we must examine the two situations one at a time.

The universe was not created by putting ingredients together. There were no ingredients. Before the Creation or The Big Bang there was no time because there was nothing to change from or into. And when the universe comes to an end there will be no matter, no possibility of change, and therefore no time.

So time is not infinite. Time began with the creation of matter and it will end when there is no matter again.

As Harry Hotspur said on his deathbed in Shakespeare's Henry IV Part 1:

But thought's the slave of life, and life time's fool
And time that takes survey of all the world
Must have a stop.

So our survey of past, present and future does not pretend to cover infinite time. It begins when time began and ends when time stops. For human purposes there is plenty of time left. A problem only arises when we waste it.

Of course you can only waste future time assuming you have free will to do one thing or another. Our primary objective should be to make better use of future time than people did in the past, so we must first reconsider the past.

Human memory is fallible. One person can have the same experience as another and remember it differently. A written record is more accurate but historians can only report what they think they have seen or what they believe they have learned from previous literature. As additional information becomes available, history changes to take it into account. That process will go on indefinitely.

The fact that written history is constantly under review does of course not mean that any of the actual events can ever change. The past is set in stone, so to speak, as the fossil record is set in stone. No one can change it. Everything in the past is forever determined.

The realization that the past is now determined led to the supposition that perhaps it had been predetermined from the beginning but there is no reason to accept predestination in respect of the past nor of the future. History is the story of events, some of which were caused by natural forces, some by the exercise of free will and some by both. Some events may not have been caused by anything at all for all we know, but once they have occurred they become part of the past. That is the difference between the past and the future. The past can never be changed. The future has not happened yet but it cannot be predestined because nothing we can identify in the past was predestined. It could have turned out one way or the other, and that can certainly be said of the future.

However the past came to be formed, we cannot travel back in time. That is not because we have not yet invented a time machine. It is because it would be a logical impossibility. If we went back to be present at the Battle of Hastings, it would not be the Battle of Hastings which we have read about, because we would then be there. Suppose we were killed, what would happen to the people we had left in the future?

If we could travel back we could take with us a fully equipped brigade of the 101st Airborne. They could stop William the Conqueror on the beaches and change the entire course of human history. In fact, the slightest change to anything in the past, other than what actually happened, would make it impossible to refer to history. You cannot be and not be at the same time. You cannot be here and somewhere else at the same time. That is logic and we are all bound by it, though verbally we may pretend not to be if we wish.

When we deny logic we not only accept two contradictory statements but we destroy language; we destroy communication. What can a word convey to someone else if in our own mind it can describe two incompatible situations? What if the past could become the future, and the future become something which happened long ago? That way madness lies.

In A Brief History of Time, Professor Hawking examined the possibility that at the end of time it would not stop but would roll back, putting into reverse everything that had ever happened. Shattered glass would reconstitute itself into the original receptacle which had broken, and time would go into reverse until, presumably, the beginning of time. After a great deal of mathematical speculation Professor Hawking demonstrated to his complete satisfaction that the entire hypothesis had been invalid. Time could not roll backwards. It was not made clear whether Professor Hawking had ever believed that it might, but that is normal for a scientific hypothesis. Many people of course are not convinced by Professor Hawking's final conclusion and prefer to keep the question open, particularly in Hollywood. But for all practical purposes we can assume that time is a succession of changes, all in one direction, some of which involve the intervention of human free will.

Omar Khayyam, a Persian poet translated by Edward Fitzgerald, wrote one verse which all children should be taught:

> **The moving finger writes; and having writ**
> **Moves on: nor all your piety nor wit**
> **Shall lure it back to cancel half a line**
> **Nor all your tears wash out a word of it.**

The future is different. Whether mathematicians or ordinary people, no-one can know with certainty in advance what in fact will happen in the future. The good news is that we have every opportunity to influence the final result and to make happen whatever it is that we want to happen.

How can that be, if nothing about the future can be known with certainty? The answer is probability theory. Some things are more likely than others. Consider a scale of zero to ten, on which ten represents absolute certainty. Zero is the score which would be given to a future event which is believed to be absolutely impossible. A rating of five means that we have no reason to suppose that a future event is likely or unlikely; it is 50:50, exactly between the areas of possibility and probability.

Everyone believes that the sun will rise tomorrow but one day it will not. The arrival of tomorrow cannot be given a rating of 10 but is so close to it that in terms of human imagination there is no difference. Nevertheless, with all human activity it is preferable to avoid the use of the term certain.

Similarly, no future event should be considered impossible, but many are close to it and would be very difficult to achieve.

Why do some people achieve much better results than others? It is because they do not set themselves any objective which is close to zero and usually they judge the probability to be greater than 5. They choose their objectives and a time frame in accordance with their own capacity, judged by their previous performance. They set objectives which are difficult to achieve but not improbable. They do not like to fail. They want to enjoy the feeling of solving problems and overcoming difficulties and they like to experience that feeling frequently, at least once each year in most cases. They always look for help wherever they are most likely to find expertise and similar previous experience. And they recognize and correct their mistakes more rapidly and more habitually than non-achievers.

Can everyone learn to be a better achiever? The short answer is yes, if they adopt the same attitudes and dedication as the habitual achievers. But first, and above all, they must be convinced that they live in a world of free will and not of determinism. That is perhaps the major difference between Islam and other religious denominations. Muslims are generally supposed to be very much on the fatalist side. Their political and military leaders believe that they can survive only if they convince their followers that there is no uncertainty in these matters. They cannot compromise because there is a universal longing for certainty. We can perhaps move to closer understanding with them by admitting that Christianity has by no means resolved these questions for its own followers.

The last sixteen books of the Old Testament of The Bible were written by prophets. None of their prophecies have come true yet and some cannot come true because they contradict each other.

Only three prophets mentioned the coming of Christianity and then in very general terms. Verses 6 and

7 of Isiah Chapter 9 read as follows, according to the King James version of The Bible:

> For unto us a child is born, unto us a son is given; and the government shall be upon his shoulder; and his name shall be called Wonderful, Counseller, The mighty God, The everlasting Father, The Prince of Peace.

> Of the increase of his government and peace there shall be no end, upon the Throne of David, and upon his kingdom, to order it and to establish it and with justice henceforth even for ever. The zeal of the Lord of hosts will perform this.

Verses 13 and 14 of Daniel Chapter 7 read as follows, without reference to Isiah:

> I saw in the night visions, and behold, one like the Son of man came with the clouds of heaven, and came to the Ancient of days, and they brought him near before him.
> And there was given him dominion, and glory, and a kingdom, that all people, nations, and languages should serve him; his dominion is an everlasting dominion, which shall not pass away, and his kingdom that which shall not be destroyed.

Chapter 4 of The Book of Micah prophesied that in the last days, nations will not lift up sword against nation, neither shall they learn war anymore.

And in Chapter 5, Verse 2, Micah predicted that the ruler of Israel would come from Bethlehem Ephratah "though thou be little among the thousands of Judah." That is perhaps the most accurate forecast in all of the Books of the Prophets, but it can hardly be used in support of the belief, once commonly held, that the New Testament simply records the fulfilment of ancient Jewish prophecies. The rulers of Israel continued to be ordinary people to the present day and we still do not have a world government.

Astrology has always been a popular pastime but it is inconsistent with a belief in free will. If the stars control your destiny you cannot change it. And why is anyone interested in knowing in advance what cannot be changed? Presumably it is because people think that prior knowledge will somehow assist them to change it – which is self-contradictory. If you are warned of a mortal danger and decide not to make a journey, you will survive but then what was it that the prophet had foreseen? Nothing happened which could have been foreseen. Better than studying the Zodiac would be concentrating on being careful when crossing the road.

The mental processes of Christian people may not be as different from Muslim processes as we have been given to understand. Let us give some more thought to this possibility.

———⚬⅂ᴐ———

CHRISTIANITY AND ISLAM

Christians believe that Jesus is The Son of God and simultaneously an equal member of the Holy Trinity. From all of the evidence we can accept the fact that Jesus was unique. As a man on earth he preached a morality and social conduct which had never been considered before and which went far beyond the Jewish capacity to understand.

When Jesus went to John the Baptist and asked to be baptized, he cut himself off from orthodox Jewry. And when he was asked "Who is my neighbour?" Jesus answered, in effect, "everyone". It was impossible for the High Priest to accept that because it would have made everyone equal in the sight of God, so what would happen to the Chosen People? An even greater problem arose when his disciple Peter declared to Jesus that he was the Christ, the son of the living God. The Jewish hierarchy had imagined someone totally different would eventually come down to earth in glory, not an unknown itinerant preacher. They never changed their minds about that. They also refused to support the crowds who proposed to crown Jesus as King of the Jews. That would have been an act of rebellion against the Roman Empire, which no-one, including Jesus, wanted at that time.

To sell everything you have and give all of your money to the poor does not appeal to rich people. They could only do it once and would then add to the poverty problem for everyone else. And how many people can indefinitely turn the other cheek? How many people can forgive an injury not seven times, but seventy times seven? Who can truly love their enemies if in return they do not become friends? Jesus was a pacifist. He did not resist arrest and he did not attempt to answer charges against him which he believed to be false.

These were very interesting ideas but practically no-one wanted to take them up. One day the world may move in that direction but that day is still far distant. The Christianity which was firmly based on the teaching of Jesus died with him. It was replaced by Pauline Christianity, which has very little to do with Jesus the Man.

Saul was of Hebrew descent. He joined the army and became a Roman citizen. He persecuted the Christians. On the road to Damascus he saw a bright light overhead and became converted. He was the first born – again and changed his name to Paul.

Paul was extremely successful as a missionary in Asia Minor and eventually as far afield as Rome. He spoke in the name of Jesus but he had very different views. We know from his letters to the cities he had converted that he was an intensely practical man. Perhaps that was the secret of his success.

Paul was not a pacifist. He was prepared to fight for his beliefs and presumably never lost his skills as a soldier. He did not make the same impossible demands on his followers as Jesus had done. Paul was an anti-feminist, as all men were in those days, with the exception of Jesus of course. Paul said Better marry than burn.

Jesus listened to criminals and said Go and sin no more. That clearly establishes his belief in free will. But Paul referred all sin to 'The Old Adam'. The inheritors of Original Sin could experience shame and regret but they could hardly be blamed by the Deity who was supposed to have invented it. Paul's solution was to rely on the redemptive power of Jesus. He did not precisely say "Go and sin as much as you like; the sacrifice of Jesus will wash your sins as white as snow if only you believe in him". But that is the message everyone received. It made Pauline Christianity very popular because it strongly implied that the past can be changed. Nevertheless, Paul tends towards determinism and removes a great deal of personal responsibility for the outcome of each life on this earth.

A problem then arose for people wishing to prepare themselves for the Last Judgement: Do they do everything possible to obey the Ten Commandments? Or do they try to follow the teaching of Jesus, impossibly difficult as it may seem to be? Or do they accept their fate as the sons of Adam and rely on Pauline Christianity to put everything right in the end?

The last chapter of the New Testament of the Bible was written by St. John the Divine. It might have been expected to answer those questions because it is called The Revelation but it does not. Like St. Paul, John the Divine claims to speak in the name of Jesus but it is impossible to believe that Jesus would have approved of any of The Revelation text. Chapter 4 begins as follows:

After this I looked, and behold, a door was opened in heaven; and the voice which I heard was as it were of a trumpet talking with me; which said, Come up hither, and I will show these things which must be hereafter.

And immediately I was in the spirit; and behold, a throne was set in heaven, and one sat on the throne. And before the throne there was a sea of glass like unto a crystal; and in the midst of the throne and round about the throne, were four beasts full of eyes before and behind.

And the first beast was like a lion, and the second beast like a calf, and the third beast had a face as a man, and the fourth beast was like a flying eagle.

And the four beasts had each of them six wings about him; and they were full of eyes within, and they rest not day and night saying Holy, holy, holy, Lord God Almighty, which was, and is to come.

Every description of heaven in The Revelation is concerned with beasts and angels and elders clothed in white. No reference is made to the people from earth or which tests they had passed to get there. Chapter 21 begins as follows:

And I saw a new heaven and a new earth; for the first heaven and the first earth were passed away; and there was no more sea.

And I, John, saw the holy city, new Jerusalem, coming down from God out of heaven, prepared as a bride adorned for her husband.

That verse gave rise to the thought that heaven might come down to earth and the people would not need to ascend to heaven after all. But John does not explain what was wrong with the old earth or the old heaven, nor whether the criteria had changed in respect of entry to heaven or hell. There is no mention of a new hell. John does prophesy that the stars will fall on the earth like

olives shaken from an olive tree. Chapter 5 refers to a
book, possibly belonging to the Recording Angel:

> **And I saw in the right hand of him that
> sat on the throne a book written within
> and on the backside, sealed with seven
> seals...**

> **And I beheld, and, lo, in the midst of the
> throne and of the four beasts, and in the
> midst of the elders, stood a Lamb as it
> had been slain, having seven horns and
> seven eyes, which are the Seven Spirits
> of God sent forth into all the earth.**

The Lamb was authorized to open the book but John
does not say what was in it. That appears to be the origin of Jesus being described as the Lamb of God, which
"Hast redeemed us to God by thy blood out of every kin-
dred, and tongue, and people, and nation; And last made
us unto our God kings and priests; and we shall reign on
the earth." Which of course, Jesus had specifically stated
he did not want to do. Just as St. Francis renounced all
wealth and is nevertheless commemorated by a magnifi-
cent palace at Assisi, Jesus was to become a dictator.

Chapter 13 of The Revelation introduces the Beast,
whose number is six hundred threescore and 6 (Not one
of the four beasts in heaven):

> **And I stood upon the sand of the sea and
> saw a beast rise up out of the sea, having**

**seven heads and ten horns, and upon his
horns ten crowns, and upon his heads
the name of blasphemy.**

**And the beast which I saw was like unto
a leopard, and his feet were as the feet of
a bear, and his mouth as the mouth of a
lion: and the dragon gave him his power,
and his seal, and great authority.**

**And I saw one of the heads as it were
wounded to death: and his deadly wound
was healed: and all the world wondered
after the beast.**

People reading The Revelation today could be for-
given for suspecting that St. John the Divine was a rav-
ing lunatic. The Revelation was included in the Bible by
mistake if it was intended to add to our knowledge of
Christianity. We can admire Mohammed for leaving it
out of the Koran. St. John, incidentally, did not prophesy
the coming of Mohammed, as far as we know.

Our St. John, whether divine or not, was extremely
sensitive to criticism:

**And if any man shall take away from
the words of the book of this prophecy,
God shall take away his part out of the
book of life, and out of the holy city, and
from the things which are written in this
book.**

**He which testifieth these things saith,
Surely I come quickly. Amen.**

This is the only reference to the means of getting to heaven or not getting there. The Koran provides more guidance than St. John the Divine but whether it is more believable is a matter for each individual to decide.

The Muslim Paradise may or may not also be the Christian Heaven. It is the conviction that it exists which creates the impression of religious unanimity and causes so many individuals to be determined to go there, one way or another. No-one likes to be left out.

In the hope that this remarkable coincidence of view can reduce the animosity between Christians and Muslims, we should examine it more closely.

—ojo—

THE AFTER LIFE

The history of religious beliefs throughout the known world is summarized in Frazer's Golden Bough. Each new religion discarded some of the earlier beliefs and adopted others. A common factor proved to be the universal belief in an after life. Religious leaders persuaded their followers that their death would not be the end of everything. They did not need much persuading. They were desperate to believe it.

The Romans expected to be ferried over the River Styx when they died, and to take up some sort of existence in the underworld. That was not where the gods lived. The Greek and Roman gods lived in the sky but they spent much of their time on earth, mingling freely with human beings. They took part in wars which they did not always win. They fell in love with some of the mortal women and the husbands were in no position to object. Their attitude was well expressed by Shakespeare:

As flies to wanton boys are we to the gods
They kill us for their sport.

The idea of becoming immortal and living on equal terms with the gods was much more attractive than the underworld. It was adopted by all religions and in due course by all forms of monotheism. There are still differences of opinion concerning the best way of getting to Heaven or Paradise and very little agreement about what we will do there but the fact of immortality seems to most people indisputable.

You may earn your place in Heaven by saintly behaviour, above average performance, trying your best or a death-bed repentance. If everyone could meet one or other of these criteria, they would all go to Heaven, which would make the entire exercise of life on earth somewhat pointless. They could have gone straight to Heaven without it, or possibly remained happily in the Garden of Eden.

That problem was solved by granting immortality to everybody but creating a place other than Heaven which would be the destination of all of the poor souls who failed to reach the required level of performance during their life on earth. It was accepted that being kept out of Heaven would be a great disappointment amounting to an extreme form of punishment, but there seemed to be no alternative. The existence of the other place would provide maximum motivation and presumably raise the general level of morality and personal triumph over adversity.

To avoid injustice it was agreed that there would have to be a Day of Judgement, at which every aspect of the life of each man and woman would be taken into account. A record would be kept by a Recording Angel of every word spoken, every action taken, every temptation resisted and every departure from the moral code, by every human being from birth to death. On the basis of those records a decision would be taken by the Supreme Being or his representative at the Gates of Heaven.

In addition to being considered omnipotent God became considered omniscient. He had to know everything that had ever happened and remember every detail of it forever. That would hardly be possible if God were sometimes absent from the scene of crimes so it was decided by the theologians that God must also be omnipresent. But God had to be present everywhere all the time without giving rise to Pantheism which is strictly forbidden as the worship of false gods.

It seemed doubtful whether the Last Judgement would be happily accepted by the people who failed the test, however comprehensive the fact-finding had been. After all, justice does not necessarily follow from a consideration of all the facts. Moreover, there would be no possibility of appeal and no explanation of the sentence once the judgement had been made. How would each individual be convinced that justice had been done? Such questions were raised but never answered.

Nevertheless, the entire theological structure was enthusiastically accepted, almost throughout the world. It provided the one thing which all human beings so desperately craved – certainty. Every authority they read or listened to, including judges, governments, kings and emperors, confirmed that there was no shadow of doubt about the after life. It was a great relief to everyone to know that something was going to continue although they did not know precisely what would happen when earthly life ended. There are two separate theories:

One is that no-one will go to Heaven until the end of the world. Everyone who has passed the test will enter Heaven together, perhaps outside time because change-less. That seems more fair than judging some people before the comparative results are all in. On the other hand, the thought of waiting indefinitely in some sort of limbo is not likely to provide as great a motivation to good works as going directly to Heaven without delay. That is what most people believe and why should they not? There is no information in the Bible about the time sequence.

Almost everything we know about the after life we learned from the poets, notably Danté Alighieri and John Milton. They were not professional theologians but no-one contradicts them on the subject of Heaven and Hell. They may be right but they did not resolve any of the customary objections.

Assuming you go straight to Heaven, what age do you expect to be? Not, presumably, an immature young rebel and not, hopefully, at the end of Shakespeare's Seventh Age of Man. A composite of your best years would be desirable, providing you were still recognizable to your-self and the friends who join you. Some people would be satisfied if only their soul survived but it is commonly believed that the body will be resurrected as well, though with no human weaknesses, no headaches, no bad temper. What ages your children will be if they arrive at the same place, raises another series of questions.

There is no marriage in Heaven but each religion imagines some sort of idyllic existence, perfect happiness and fond recollections of the world below. That will be the reward for a lifetime of hardship and it will go on for ever. There is no indication in the Bible about social relationships in the after life or what you will all be doing but there will be no disappointment.

Everyone agrees that rich men should not easily ascend to Heaven. They have been rewarded sufficiently in this world, in the opinion of poor people, no matter how well they may score on the tests. One reason for excluding them is the belief that money can never be made honestly. So if you are rich you must do more to compensate.

In every religion the stick is much more clearly defined than the carrot. The descent into Hell has been described in hideous detail since time immemorial and must surely have produced some improvement in human behaviour. Whether it stimulates belief in an all-powerful, merciful and just deity may be open to doubt. But there it is. The sins of the guilty will not be expiated because Hell like Heaven, will go on for ever.

The favourite joke of King George VI concerned the Scottish Presbyterian minister who despaired of his congregation and preached hellfire every Sunday morning. You're all damned, he would shout. And when you are toiling and moiling in the bottomless pit of Hell, you will raise your eyes to Heaven and say Lord! Lord! We didna' ken. And the Lord in his infinite mercy and compassion will look down and say – Well ye ken the noo!"

The fact remains that we do not know yet. Why does everyone want to be certain there is an after life, when for perhaps two thirds of the human race it is expected to be damnation? Why do we not come to the conclusion that Heaven and Hell are both poetic inventions and do not exist at all? All we would be losing is our sense of certainty, which is in any case an illusion.

And that perhaps would be a good starting point for reconciliation in the Middle East. It is an illusion for Muslims as well as for the Western democracies. Let us all talk about it together.

—⚭—

CHAPTER TWENTY-ONE

THE PRESENT

Something important was left out of the discussion of an unchangeable past and a future involving free-will. The past consists of records and memories. The future does not yet exist because it has not happened yet. The past ends at the moment when the future begins. So does the present not exist at all?

Most people think they are living in the present. That does no harm if they mean they are mainly interested in the fairly recent past and the fairly near future. Life after all does not go on for very long. But everything we do takes time. Time cannot stand still, whatever was thought to have happened when Joshua defeated the Amorites.

If we spend two hours reading history, we will find that when we have finished reading, the day is two hours later than when we started. We were not in fact living in the past, we were using the present and the future to review records and memories from the past.

If we receive a letter and send a reply by return of mail there is necessarily a passage of time while we go to the desk, find pen and paper, write the letter, address the envelope, put on a stamp and walk to the mailbox. That was all in the past by the time our letter dropped out of our hand; it was no longer in the present for us. It existed, probably, as part of the future for the person who had not yet received the letter. The present is a very short length of time, if in fact it has a time dimension.

We cannot entirely agree with Shakespeare's clown in Twelfth Night;

> **What is love? 'tis not hereafter**
> **Present mirth hath present laughter,**
> **What's to come is still unsure;**
> **In delay there lies no plenty,**
> **Then come kiss me, sweet and twenty**
> **Youth's a stuff will not endure.**

Shakespeare is taking the common sense view that the present is a series of packages of time. He is aware that the laughter must follow the joke; we say that it must follow immediately. To Feste it is still part of the present.

In this song, Shakespeare confirms the transitory nature of life. Everything after youth is in the future but it will come very soon. Make the most of every minute. And Shakespeare clearly accepts that the future cannot be known with certainty.

Macbeth, who had brought himself to ruin and knew he was close to death, realized that time is continuous in one direction only. For him the whole of life was an hour, though it seems very slow in passing.

> **Tomorrow, and tomorrow, and tomorrow,**
> **Creeps in this petty pace from day to day**
> **To the last syllable of recorded time**

And all our yesterdays have lighted fools
The way to dusty death. Out, out, brief can-
dle!
Life's a walking shadow, a poor player
That struts and frets his hour upon the stage
And then is heard no more; it is a tale
Told by an idiot, full of sound and fury
Signifying nothing.

Before we invented clocks the working day was from dawn to dusk. The year was measured by the agricultural seasons, different in every part of the world and changing with climatic conditions. The present was a term used differently by everybody and never properly defined. People still refer to "'the present day'", meaning "'in our own time'". And "'at the present time'", meaning recently. Military men confirm their presence by reporting "'All present and correct'", meaning "'for the time being you can count on our presence'".

The Romans divided their days into twelve equal hours, which varied according to the season; the first hour began at sunrise, the seventh at noon, and the twelfth ended at sunset. In midsummer, each hour was about 75 minutes long; in midwinter, about 45 minutes. Towards the eighth hour (2pm) all business stopped.

The working day is now a worldwide inter-relationship of businessmen and financiers communicating instantaneously and independently of the time shown on the clocks in each location. That today is the present, the dividing line between past and future events.

A line appears to be continuous, whether it is a straight line or a curve. Mathematicians, however, see a line as a succession of points infinitesimally close. That is the way to visualize the passage of time.

To influence the future we must exercise our free will continuously. The only alternative is to watch events as they occur and hope that they will not affect us adversely. In that case our life could just as well be governed by determinism.

The continuity of time is simply a reflection of the fact that the earth is continuously turning on its axis, creating day and night at different times everywhere. And the earth is continuously traveling round the sun, creating the seasons at different times everywhere. Nevertheless we can calculate our position at any one point of time with a fair degree of accuracy. Our position in space is constantly changing but we can always know where we are now. That is what the present means – now, at this particular moment, but moving fast.

To combine economic and political resources for the benefit of humanity in these circumstances is not an easy task. In fact it is an objective which is as ambitious as anyone could reasonably set themselves. That is the objective which we must try to share with out Muslim friends. It is difficult but feasible and will benefit all of us.

An apparent objection to this common-sense acceptance of the continuity of time is a view expressed by many, if not all, of modern space scientists. They provide a convincing case that the light from distant stars began its journey millions of years ago. From this fact they argue that people on earth are seeing other galaxies as they were millions of years ago. We are today, they pretend, seeing a star as it was in its own present, which is not ours.

When we look at a photograph we see something now which looks more or less as it was many years ago but that does not mean that we are being physically transported back into the past. When light from a star enters our eyes it is now, and it is now for everyone everywhere. We must make what we will of it but it is our present and it is the present of every star. The age of the universe is everywhere the same.

Ignore the absurdity of multiple universes. They were invented by people with too much time on their hands.

Specialists must step back occasionally and review their relationship with the rest of humanity. Global men and women must be all-rounders; as many were in the Age of Enlightenment. We must consider all subjects, not just one or two. That is the secret of the well balanced mind.

———ᴼᴸᵒ———

BAND OF BROTHERS

There is no longer credibility in the dream of world government, if in fact there ever was. Even with all the information systems, instantaneous communications and unlimited wealth, no central authority could satisfy the myriad incompatible demands for welfare simultaneously with freedom and human rights. Democracy has gone too far for that. What alternatives are there?

The European Union is a loose association of sovereign states. Not as loose as the United Nations perhaps but comparable. Even if the draft E.U. Constitution had been accepted unanimously it would have been a pale imitation of the American Constitution. Rejection by the people of France and Holland confirmed a total lack of support for a United States of Europe, much to the relief of England.

Each separate state of the enlarged Union is responsible for its own internal security, covered in America by the enormous Department of Homeland Security. Presumably we can expect reasonable collaboration in Europe but there will be no single authority. The immigration policy of every nation-state is a matter for its own government to decide, and to change whenever it wishes. That is what sovereignty means.

The North American Treaty Organization still exists. It is appropriate to deal with the threat of international war on a grand scale and depends almost entirely on the military might of America. That is not thought to affect sovereignty because no-one believes there is any danger of international war in Europe. The European countries are spending no more than the minimum required to satisfy national pride and provide for military parades. Costs may increase if troops are needed to maintain internal security but not for international wars as far as we can see. Europe does not want any obligations and resents America for assuming them when the United Nations Organization chooses to do nothing.

That is perhaps the reason for anti-American feeling in Europe and regrettably, in Canada. It does not seem rational because no-one is being made to do anything they do not want to do. America called on Europe for volunteers in Iraq and answer came there none, or almost none. America was forced to act unilaterally or stay at home and hope for the best. The notable exceptions were Australia, New Zealand and England, although it made Tony Blair unpopular with all political parties in London including his own.

So how do we prosecute war against terrorists? Can we rely on the United Nations if we are patient enough? Certainly not. They have taken not a single step in that direction. Member states will do whatever they can at home, one suicide bomber at a time, and try to keep a low profile.

Are there no countries to take a broader view? No institutions and no individuals who want to look after the world and not simply their own selfish interests? Yes, there are some, and there have been for a long time, but they have little or no political influence. Well then, perhaps we should identify them and give them some support.

For more than two centuries the Royal Navy maintained the freedom of the seas. The Admiralty directed ships to the farthest outposts of empire, to keep the shipping lanes open for trade and commerce in times of peace and for the transport of troops, whenever required, which was fairly often. The British Government, of course, paid for all of the vessels under orders from London.

But that is not all the naval captains did. They waged a continuous war against pirates in the Mediterranean, the Indian Ocean and the Malay Straits among other places. They captured cargoes reported to be stolen and took them to port. They stopped vessels carrying smuggled armaments and dangerous drugs. They stopped the slave trade wherever they found it and set the slaves free. In fact they kept the high seas open for the legitimate trade of all nations and not only in support of imperial interests.

Of course the naval officers had to be sensible and use discretion in their contacts with other jurisdictions. There is no record of courts martial in respect of having exceeded their official duties, and no charges by other nations of illegal seizure. All mariners going about their rightful occupations were pleased to see naval vessels. There was usually no-one else to look after them.

For most of the nineteenth century the US Navy was almost fully occupied with the enforcement of the Monroe Doctrine in continental waters. America accepted the activities of the Royal Navy elsewhere in the world, including the imposition of British law governing the slave trade. In addition the United States Navy opened up Japan and the Philippines and captured some of the Algerian pirates, so they have had plenty of good experience.

In World War II of course there was complete collaboration between all of the navies of the English speaking democracies. The Australian and New Zealand navies remained separate but totally devoted to the Pacific War under the leadership of General MacArthur.

General Eisenhower was appointed Supreme Commander of the Normandy Invasion because that was the way to win the war. There was no mention of national sovereignty on D Day.

That is the relationship we should revive today. If we speak English and if we agree we are all equally threatened, what we need for ultimate victory is a united front, as we have demonstrated so frequently in the past.

Piracy is on its way to becoming a major industry again. Let us begin with that problem. Piracy may be considered as a form of terrorism on the high seas so it does not directly involve the United Nations nor member states concerned with their own territorial integrity. Declaring war on pirates will avoid legal problems which cause so much expense and loss of time. We cannot assume that a pirate is innocent until proven guilty beyond all doubt in a court of law and in several different languages. He must be captured without delay and kept out of the piracy business, much like the terrorists who believe in jihad.

Piracy must be stopped. That will be done if democratic governments authorize their navies to stop it. They must then provide the ships and information systems and after that, leave the navies to do their duty.

No-one will want to stop that process as no-one wanted to stop it before. Every ally and every threatened country will collaborate with a central control system in each ocean. They will provide access to the best ports in the world, including Singapore, Jakarta, Penang, Trincomalee, Mumbai and Karachi. And why not Hong Kong and Shanghai? Who could refuse the invitation to work closely with the Chinese navy in the pursuit of pirates?

At least we should give them all the opportunity to refuse. They will not refuse. They are at their wits end how to deal with pirates. Fortunately, all of their vessels and naval personnel are organized on the British model and on every ship there is someone who speaks English.

It so happens that all of the navies of the English speaking democracies descend directly from the British

Admiralty and training colleges. Canada, Australia, New Zealand and of course America itself, inherited the skills passed down from Nelson and the great navigators and explorers celebrated in history. There is a brotherhood of the sea. Personal ties have been preserved through war and peace and are still very much alive to this day. Naval training colleges are all practically identical. They value tradition above everything.

Stories of English by David Crystal (Penguin Books 2004) is a superb history of the language. Incredible detail. On page 445 Crystal reproduces a letter sent by a West African king to a naval officer in 1842.

"To Commander Raymond.

Now we settle treaty for not sell slaves, I must tell you something, I want your queen to do for we. Now we can't sell slaves again, we must have too much man for country, and want something for make work and trade, and if we could get seed for cotton and coffee we could make trade. Plenty sugar cane live here, and if some man come teach we way for do it we get plenty sugar too, and then some man must come for teach book proper, and make all men saby God like white man, and then we go on for same fashion. We thank you too much for what thing you come do for keep thing right. Long time we no look Man-of-war as Blount promise, and one

Frenchman come make plenty palaver for slave when he can't get them. You been do very proper for we, and now we want to keep proper mouth. I hope some Man-of-war come some time with proper captain all same you to look out and help we keep word when French man-of-war come. What I want for dollar side is fine coat and sword all same I tell you and the rest in copper rods. I hope Queen Victoria and young prince will live long time, and we get good friend. Also I want bomb and shell.

I am, your best friend,
King Eyamba V, 'King of all Black Man'.23

The letter displays a number of distinctive grammatical abbreviations and substitutions as well as some lexical features (saby 'savvy', palaver 'talk') typical of an emerging pidgin, though it is unclear just how far texts of this kind, which are extremely variable in their language, can be said to be the precursors of modern pidgins."

We would not mind a letter like this today in response to our request to use foreign harbours for anti-piracy vessels.

David Crystal's mind-set is supportive of all dialects but in the end he agrees with us that a standard written language would be an improvement.

If piracy is allowed to flourish it will be equivalent to the collapse of law and order on dry land. It will affect even greater quantities of trade and freedom of movement than threats to air travel. So why not start there? Anti-piracy patrols will pick up illegal oil and armament shipments. Drug smuggling is already on the list of world emergencies. Slave trading is coming back, not on the previous massive scale but undoubtedly beyond the ability of the United Nations to control. Build on the freedom of the seas and other forms of international co-operation will follow. And who knows? We may even pick up a few genuine terrorists en route to somewhere.

Every government with the exception of America has reduced the size of its fleet because it is no longer necessary or cannot be fitted into shrunken defence budgets. Enforcing freedom of the seas will not require additional battleships or cruisers or submarines. A few more destroyers and frigates perhaps, but mainly small high speed heavily armed boats with all of the latest technology. They were called gunboats when they were sent up the rivers in the days of empire. In WWII they were the coastal forces of the Royal Naval Volunteer Reserve. Very easy to reconstitute in every major waterway of the world.

The British fleet as well as the army had no problem cooperating with the US forces in Iraq. Canadian vessels also made a contribution to the control of illicit shipments of oil and armaments. Australia and New Zealand naval vessels have always been at the disposal of America since General Macarthur arrived at Port Moresby in an MTB from Manila. All that is required today is the approval and financial contribution from each government that wishes to participate.

One major step forward would be an agreement to avoid all reference to national sovereignty. The only people with sovereign power today are the terrorists and pirates.

Women do not like war but they like terrorism less. We need not expect any gender problems from globalization. Virginia Woolf wrote this many years ago:

"As a woman I have no country. As a woman my country is the whole world."

CHAPTER TWENTY-THREE

THE ENVIRONMENT

A decision to reduce or avoid a particular activity because it affects the environment is not very rational. Everything affects the environment. Everything is the environment.

American law presently requires unlimited effort and expenditure to avoid the extinction of any living organism. That is not restricted to elephants, tigers, seals and other loveable creatures. It includes every present survivor from creation or evolution or whatever brought it into existence.

The legislation was no doubt passed with the support of religious people who believe that nothing God created should ever disappear if human kind can prevent it. They probably accept the fact that 30,000 species become extinct every single year but man must forget all other priorities if anything can be done to save the spotted owl, or whatever is next on the list.

This is perhaps the most ineffective law ever promulgated. That may seem a savage criticism of the United States Congress but in the present context there is no time for diplomatic niceties.

Then we have global warming; the possibility that New York will be flooded unless we build dykes like the

Dutch; the fact of glaciers melting and the likelihood that the Gulf Stream will get colder and freeze Britain out; reducing carbon emissions by adding methanol to gasoline, although making methanol uses more energy than can be saved in the car exhaust. And so on.

Every scientist who studies these matters has a provisional view of the cause/effect relationships; the apparent priorities; the most likely set of solutions; and his own personal feelings. There is no general agreement at the moment. That is because the relation of our earth to the sky is an extremely complex study which we only began recently. When the scientists produce a convincing hypothesis, or when only half of them do, we should take their advice. In the meantime we should continue to create the wealth which they will eventually need for investment in environmental engineering.

Public demonstrations do not contribute to democratic decision-making. When thousands of people walk down the street they have no common understanding, no solution to the problem, no policy and no way of implementing it if they had. The fears and emotions expressed are the result of almost total ignorance. Nevertheless, we should let them march.

When we get more down to earth, naturally we are on firmer ground. That is to say, closer to productive business management. We should review all of our firmly held convictions in the light of present day cost/benefit analysis.

Nineteenth-century economists believed that land represented a special measure of value. Land seemed to be permanent, indestructible and immovable; infinitely divisible; impossible to steal; useful as the locations of towns, villages, mining, sheep farming, agriculture, gardening, hunting and aesthetic pursuits. Before the industrial revolution the one stable and enduring economic value appeared to be rent from the land.

Now we can change land physically by the use of explosives and bulldozers. We can improve land for agricultural purposes by irrigation and fertilizers. We can add greatly to its value by building cities and airports on it. We can destroy its value for all practical purposes by pollution or by permitting the soil to erode or to lose essential ingredients.

Land is therefore like any other factor of production. We can use it intelligently and economically and efficiently to produce goods and services without adversely affecting our social environment. Or we can use land in a thoughtless, wasteful and unintelligent way, leaving us eventually with loss instead of profit; famine instead of feast; and bare rock instead of field and forest.

Until recently, air was considered to be a free good. No matter how much air was used by people or industries there was never any scarcity, so air had no economic value. At the bottom of a mine or in a submarine a shortage could occur but almost everyone took for granted that fresh air would always be universally available. Even in those days it was realised that air can become polluted by industrial processes and by the internal combustion engine. The cost of removing soot and particulates deposited on buildings and clothes was accepted however reluctantly by the people concerned. There was no way of avoiding the occurrence of air pollution, short of stopping the productive processes which were creating wealth for everyone. Even health problems were accepted as being a necessary result of the economic system and not the fault of particular companies.

Today there is a general recognition that excessive air pollution has to be controlled and if possible reduced, no matter the economic cost. A North American city of two million people will consume annually about nine million tons of coal, oil and gas for heating, plus three million tons of gasoline for cars, trucks and buses. From this combustion more than five trillion cubic feet of exhaust gases are emitted, many of them poisonous. With the gases more than 60,000 tons of dust are emitted, of which present control systems remove about 15,000 tons, or one quarter of the total particulates. The cost of installing electrostatic precipitators and other means of reducing air pollution will clearly increase significantly in the twenty first century.

A problem of almost equal significance is the economical disposal or recycling of domestic garbage. If the population of a large city is increasing at the rate of 1% per year, the evidence in North America indicates that the volume of refuse in that city will increase by 1.3 per cent per year, especially if the standard of living is rising and waste becomes more affordable. A typical North American city produces an average of 0.63 tons of garbage per year per capita, or at least 1 million tons per 2 million inhabitants. Every city is running out of acceptable sites for garbage dumps and it will become increasingly expensive to truck the garbage longer and longer distances. In any case, a properly designed garbage dump is expensive to construct and operate, requiring pipes to suck out methane gas and pump out toxic liquids which then also need a disposal system.

It is possible to compost municipal garbage by chopping it up in large grinding machines and passing it through a composting chamber with controlled intakes of air and moisture. At present the process takes about ten days but could be greatly accelerated by the controlled addition of suitable bacteria which consume the organic waste. Research is being conducted to solve the problem of heavy metals remaining in the composted material. Several European countries are operating accelerated composting plants and replacing their lost topsoil with the output. The next step will be to compost garbage with sewage sludge, which is another urban product with disposal problems. An equal weight of domestic garbage and sludge from a primary sewage treatment plant provides the ideal chemistry for accelerated composting.

Throughout our lives we have all been buying goods and services at prices which did not include any allowance for environmental impact. The standard of living all over the world has been subsidized to that extent and all we are facing is the realization that the bills are now coming in. We can choose to conserve energy and consume less to compensate for our past misuse of the environment, or we can find ways to solve the problems of production without polluting the earth, water or air. All such solutions will of course have to be paid for by governments out of taxes or by including the costs in the selling price of the products.

It is we who will suffer, and we who will benefit, whether we continue to act foolishly and short-sightedly, or whether we act wisely and in time. The loss or the profit will be ours in any case, because there is nobody here but us.

Corrective measures at the micro-economic level which can be identified and paid for out of current revenue without destroying profitability, are of course the responsibility of corporate management working closely with municipalities. Progress can be expected as soon as the facts are known and the technical capacity exists. Concentration on local obligations at that level will be far more productive than cosmic panic. We do not need simultaneous action by entire industries and we certainly do not have to wait for international treaties. Diplomatic negotiations take forever and agreements are frequently renounced without explanation when the slightest domestic difficulty arises. National sovereignty!

——⚬⅃⚬——

CHAPTER TWENTY-FOUR

GLOBALIZATION

Purchasing Agents used to buy raw materials and semi-finished products when Production Managers asked them to.

Now there are Procurement Directors with eyes and ears in every corner of the globe. They know the competitive situation of their company, now and in the longer term. They want to find out all about their competitors before their customers do. They buy just in time so they will not lock up capital unnecessarily or end up with large unusable inventories. Their worldwide surveillance identifies potential customers as well as new sources of supply.

Those are the companies which out-source complete products if it is more economical to buy than to make them in home factories. Their highest priority is to satisfy their customers. They know they cannot rely on customer loyalty. They know they will lose their business if competitors would suit them better, whether based at home or overseas.

These companies enjoy meeting new challenges and welcome new opportunities. They know that they must remain constantly flexible. When they discontinue a product line they know that their highly qualified technical staff will soon be fully occupied doing something else. They are responsible for developing their most important resource, brainpower. Employees must take control of their own careers, including their pension plans, and keep their own technologies up to date. And those companies are making more money every year.

Then there are companies who do not study world conditions or competitive developments, perhaps because they are afraid of what they would discover. They are unprepared to meet products with superior quality and lower prices. They have no defence except to ask the government for subsidies or tariff protection. They use the oldest argument against Adam Smith – infant industries. But protection ensures they will never grow up.

Perhaps it is fortunate that governments can no longer provide financial aid or tariff protection to all of the companies who claim to need help. The demographic problems facing all governments are bad enough, particularly in respect of pension obligations, without adding to future liabilities.

Governments which accept globalization and permit it to proceed without restriction will find they can continue to administer half of the wealth created by the private sector, adding we may hope, to the happiness and social contentment of the community. However, governments which see globalization as a threat to their industrial survival and perhaps to their own existence, will find that they end up with no tax revenues at all.

This sudden change from sovereignty to being virtually powerless in economic matters will come as a great shock to many electorates. How can this possibly be happening? Is everyone in the developing world better than we are at everything? How did they seem to be so backward and yet are suddenly so competitive?

The economic analysis is relatively simple but has been obscured by a general belief that things are other than they are, particularly in respect of national sovereignty. Governments and electorates must go back to school for a few minutes.

International trade can occur in three different circumstances. A country can make bicycles but cannot grow bananas for climatic reasons. Another country can grow bananas but cannot make bicycles. It is self-evident that both countries will benefit from an exchange of bicycles and bananas, otherwise neither will have both.

In the second case, both countries can make bicycles and grow bananas but one has a comparative advantage in bicycles and the other in bananas. Using smaller quantities of scarce resources they can produce the same volume of output and can then exchange goods to their mutual advantage.

An advanced industrial state with a good climate may possess a comparative advantage over another country in every form of agricultural and industrial production but it will have a greater comparative advantage in some products than others. The production they forgo in the areas of comparative disadvantage will set free scarce resources, which can be put to better use elsewhere. So even in this situation both countries can gain by exchange. There is always a rate of exchange between two products which will be beneficial to both parties when they each specialize. Comparative advantage can always be mutual advantage. That explains how very poor countries can trade with very rich countries without having to rely on foreign aid or philanthropic sentiments, provided free trade is permitted.

If wealthy countries refuse to trade with poor countries on the grounds of domestic protection, the poor countries will never become rich and may present political and military problems, as Japan did to America and Europe before WWII.

The term "level playing field" crops up from time to time. But if the playing fields were level there would be no trade. The world is looking for areas where the playing fields are least level for reasons of natural advantage but not for reasons of protection.

Thomas L. Friedman, a famous American journalist, wrote a book called The World is Flat. It was republished by Farrar, Straus and Giroux, New York, in an updated and expanded version in 2006. On almost every page there is a reference to the world being flat, or that it is flattening, although Friedman admits that some parts of the world are not likely to become flat, for a variety of reasons.

Mr. Friedman makes a strong case for globalization and the prosperity produced by the removal of tariffs and non-tariff barriers to trade, but he refers to those policies as a general levelling of the playing field. That is not the usual meaning of that catch phrase. European farmers do not want the playing field to be levelled for the benefit of others. They want to continue to be employed as farmers although their crops and their methods of farming are no longer profitable. They expect their governments to maintain an unlevel playing field in the Friedman sense.

That is typical of the misunderstandings which arise when sporting terminology is applied to economic or financial analysis. Nothing sensible can result when the analogy is false, as it almost invariably is. On Page 460 Mr. Friedman admits that he has "engaged in literary licence". "Indeed, let me go even further and make a deeper confession. I know the world is not flat". But he continues to use the phrase to the very end of the book. It greatly increases the complexity of all comparisons, especially after reading Page 470:

"There's not just the flat world and the unflat world. Many people live in a twilight zone between the two."

Fortunately, there are many valuable statements in every chapter of the book and they remain equally valid when every flat world reference is removed or ignored.

It sometimes escapes notice in the classical analysis of exchange that it does not apply only to international trade. It applies to all trade everywhere, between town and country, between two towns, between a town and a village, and between two individuals in the same village.

It is the basis of the division of labour. It is the basis of all wealth creation.

When two individuals in a village exchange their products and immediately consume them they both benefit but they do not generate investment capital. Profit does not mean simply arriving at a preferred economic position, which barter enables both parties to do. Profit means ending a transaction with a surplus, which can be used to expand and improve or diversify into further profitable transactions. That requires an entrepreneurial capacity and an on-going business philosophy.

Fruit grows on trees locally but farmers do not sell it locally if they can ship it 3,000 miles and make more money; that is to say, send it to someone who will appreciate it more. Make it where it is cheapest and sell it to whoever wants it the most.

International trade implies a continuous relationship between many such structures. Businessmen must have access to supply and demand conditions in each country of interest to them and bring the producers and potential customers together. That is the function today of the Internet. Producers have to receive a return which is sufficient to persuade them to continue in business. Importers have to cover the costs of transportation, warehousing, handling, administration and risk of loss, damage, delay and currency fluctuations. International trade must be profitable to the people organizing it. The customers have to receive good value (compared with local alternatives) otherwise the exporters will not be able to rely on repeat business. But the customers do not get any of the profit unless they resell the goods. The final consumers benefit from the exchange, as an employee benefits from exchanging his labour for wages, but only the business organization receives the profit after taxation. Without the business organization (the Phoenician trader) there would be no profit, so justice is being done, and has to be done, if the business is to continue.

That entire analytical summary related to the past as well as today. It produced an unimaginable increase in wealth but at the same time convinced the western countries that because the third world was becoming richer, they must beware of becoming poorer; even that in the long run they were in danger of losing everything they had. The brakes had to be put on. That was the political message delivered by the countries of the industrial west to the Third World and implemented through democratic processes whenever politically acceptable.

Governments had always believed they possessed unlimited political power but it had only ever been power over their own people. They could benefit some people at the expense of others and frequently did so, either for electoral reasons or because they truly believed that producers were more deserving than consumers. But power over other distant nations, now highly competitive, was more difficult to come by.

At an early stage of the Twentieth Century expansion of overseas trade, it became clear that shipping capacity would soon become inadequate. Containerization solved that problem but produced others. London Docks did not like containers so the container ships went on up the coast to Felixstowe, which is now the largest container port in the British Isles. That is what happens to Trade Unions and governments which try to impede the progress of globalization. They lose what they had.

Within national boundaries a government can control monopoly, or what appears may one day become monopoly. And in some circumstances a government may wish to form a monopoly and protect it from competition within its own borders. But in the wide world there is no monopoly. Every product is in free competition with every other product and every other industry. What good are anti-trust laws? No use at all.

And within national boundaries the state could control prices if it wanted to; also the terms and conditions of employment and trade, and legislate ten thousand miniscule regulations covering every economic activity, as the European Union is trying to do. Even imports and exports can be controlled to a certain extent.

But every form of government control of legal trade reduces the potential prosperity in total. And now fortunately, with globalization, the end of controlled trade is approaching. We are seeing our old friend national sovereignty coming to the end of its days.

Governments in future must study what will benefit the entire country and not only the traditional interest groups. And the benefit of all will be provided by the freedom of all to conduct their business as they wish, worldwide. Full circle to Adam Smith.

We will become better off if we reduce tariffs country by country, even if our trading partners do not reduce theirs. Instead of imposing dumping duties we must request other countries to send us goods and services with the lowest prices in the world. They will only continue to do so if we can continue to pay for them.

On the basis of that profitability we will deal with local unemployment by retraining, relocation and retirement as necessary. Ask the farmers to maintain a healthy countryside for a reasonable return but import our food from the countries which can produce it most economically. That is no favour to them. We will be acting in our own self-interest, as Adam Smith told us our baker was doing in 1776.

It is possible that European countries with a single national language may find it more difficult than the English speaking countries to take full advantage of globalization. Indeed it is possible that they will decide to fight globalization tooth and nail. That is their privilege.

If they do they may enjoy some short-term advantages. Demographic problems will be reduced or removed if they do not try to maintain the present level of population. The existing workforce can retire on the present terms of age and pensions. With a smaller workforce in future the salary levels should increase without changing the terms of employment too much.

There would be no point in adding to unemployment by bringing in immigrants to be housed and fed and trained, simply as a means of preserving the language. Tariffs and subsidies could be continued for a number of years in conformity with a changeless society and a changeless industrial supply and demand structure.

However the children could not prosper in such a paralysed world. They can stay at home quietly with their parents or they can learn English and contribute to globalization.

—ono—

CORPORATE GOVERNANCE

Corporations, firms and partnerships are legal persons. They are subject to the same laws and regulations as individuals are in each country. In addition they are subject to three forms of governance, all operating simultaneously:

1. Self control.
2. Tax regimes and other legislation designed to restrict certain types of economic behaviour.
3. Global governance.

Until recently in most countries, corporate governance was left to the discretion of managers and boards of directors, provided they refrained from price fixing or otherwise reducing competition. It may seem remarkable that managers and directors distributed so much revenue to the owners of land, labour and capital instead of maximizing their own incomes but that is easily explained. It is in their own long term interest to do so. Unethical behaviour or outright theft tends to remove companies from the market place. All stake holders will be adversely affected by failure, including the managers.

Generally speaking businessmen have always been honest. If they know what the law is they try to conform with it.

The exchange of goods and services which constitutes free enterprise makes it unlikely that people can enrich themselves by impoverishing others. The richer everyone else becomes, the greater the opportunity for each individual to become better off also. The distribution of wealth does not proceed evenly, and perhaps not fairly, but we all want to be in an increasingly wealthy economy and not one which is continuously shrinking. That puts us on the side of law and order, all other things being equal.

The economic and social costs of bankruptcies or frequent losses include unemployment, disillusionment, individual disappointment and international resentments. Something has happened which left one or both parties to the exchange of goods and services dissatisfied and disinclined to accept without complaint the results of the experience.

The successful business manager is consciously resolved to avoid such situations to the best of his or her ability. Every transaction may be considered to have been ethically sound if it leaves both parties well satisfied and anxious to continue their business relationship. If it leaves either party undecided whether to repeat the transaction or not, the manager has to review every aspect of the business, including what may be called ethical standards.

There is nothing subjective about such judgements. People continue to do business or they do not. No-one hesitates to use ethical terms in this context. The failure of a business is a bad thing. It is not right of management to permit the livelihood of other people to disappear through lack of forethought, laziness, or for any other reason. Executives ought not to waste resources. It is wrong to falsify the accounts. It is good to satisfy the customer. Everyone ought to have equal opportunity.

We might all agree with ethical propositions of this sort, and that would not necessarily be because they are true in any absolute sense. It is because people who do not agree with them, and who do not act as if they are true, tend to leave the scene of economic activity, or at least to become a less significant part of it.

For these reasons the globalization of business could proceed, as international commerce has done in the past, on the basis of unrestricted free enterprise. We know that world prosperity will not be achieved by remaining safely at home. Businessmen are aware of these facts and most of them do the best they can, for their sakes and for ours.

But at the end of the Twentieth Century and early in the Twenty First there was a series of spectacular bankruptcies, apparent evidence of fraud on a massive scale and unprecedented levels of payment to executives and directors including those who had been responsible for the collapse of their companies. These developments reduced public confidence in corporate governance, which in any case had never been well understood.

National governments have always been ambivalent on the subject of profit. The greater the net corporate revenue at the end of each financial year, the greater is the revenue from profit taxes. On the other hand, governments know that an increase in profit by some companies and not others in the same industry is an indication of imperfect competition. They fear that any market which is not perfectly competitive will end up as a monopoly with only one supplier. Anti-trust legislation is based on that assumption. From that point of view the less profit there is the better. To avoid facing this issue, competition departments these days are keeping a low profile.

The calculation of profit is made by the accountants employed by each company who record all revenues and expenditures and present a profit and loss statement to the tax authorities each year. It would be impossibly expensive for governments to employ enough accountants to verify the corporate statements, even on a spot check basis, so they rely on audits made by outside firms of professional accountants. Those accountants are themselves paid by the corporations they serve so the annual accounts are rarely if ever rejected or even seriously questioned. The auditors do their best on a spot check basis but they have no excuses to offer when profits prove to have been losses shortly after submission to the authorities.

It is not clear what, if anything, can be done about that. Even more ineffectual would be global governance.

Perhaps it is better to rely on the economy to remove wrong doers as, eventually, it invariably has done in the past. Self- control is much better than no control.

Corporate governance by taxation authorities is a large and complex subject. For the purposes of this book it is sufficient to point out that the responsibility for introducing share options as a means of attracting new managers was considered carefully by all tax departments and accepted as a brilliant new idea. They expected that profit would increase because all of the managers would be trying harder. They did try harder, but not to increase corporate profit. As they paid more to themselves the annual profit could only go down. In many cases it went down to zero. That was because they had only one objective – to increase the value of their shares on the stock exchange. Knowing how fickle the investing public can be, the managers cashed in their share options as rapidly as possible. Perfectly foreseeable.

One aspect which apparently escaped the notice of the inventor of share options is that investors are people who had earned money in other ways but who saved some of it, that is to say refrained from immediate consumption. The goods and services they did not consume became available to the industries serving entrepreneurs and thus provided new investment capital without causing inflation. The managers and directors who were given share options of course had not saved any money at all, so they were not part of the investing public. They were nothing but salaried members of the labour force being rewarded for nothing. Moreover, they frequently back-dated their share options, clearly an illegal proceeding. How the tax authorities could have been taken in by such an obvious misrepresentation is not clear, but it certainly reduces public confidence in the ability of tax departments to enforce acceptable corporate governance.

The Director-General of the World Trade Organization, Pascal Lamy, believes that Global Governance will become increasingly necessary because globalization has had very positive effects but also some with negative consequences. In a speech to the Chilean Government in Santiago on 30 January 2006 he listed "worrisome phenomena" as follows:

- scarcity of energy resources
- deterioration of the environment
- natural disasters
- the spread of pandemics (AIDS, bird flu)
- the ensuing complexity of analysis, forecasts and predictability (financial crisis)
- and the migratory movements provoked by insecurity, poverty or political instability, which says Mr. Lamy, are also a product of globalization.

It is to be hoped that solutions will be found to some or all of these "worrisome phenomena", by global governance or by any other means, but one thing is certain. Corrective measures will be very expensive and they can only be implemented by using some of the wealth created by globalization. If that money is used instead for

social purposes and in any way reduces the benefits provided by globalization, the worrisome phenomenae will
remain and there will be less money available for corrective purposes. That would be a sad repetition of mercantilism as opposed to free enterprise in the English sense.

The primary objective for global governance should
be the provision of a universal Rule of Law equivalent to
the maintenance of law and order in democratic states.
That may in itself meet the criteria presented by Mr.
Lamy as "Humanising Globalization".

The New American Foundation in Washington DC
believes in "A global system which will be far more
heterogeneous, cosmopolitan, liberal and flexible than
today's." That sounds just what the doctor ordered, but
a senior fellow of the Foundation, Mr. Barry Lynn, has
written in his book The End of the Line (Doubleday) that
America has the responsibility "of using state power to
engineer markets and systems to serve its own people,
while ceding to other states far more space to serve
their citizens in ways of their own choosing." And "the
American mind should be exorcised of today's mecha-
nistic utopianism," presumably describing free trade
which has not been organized by governments or trade
unions.

A desirable objective but a strange way of getting
there. Perhaps a rear-guard action by State Troopers.

Supportive evidence for globalization is provided by Robert Conquest in his book The Dragons of
Expectation, published by W.W. Norton and Company

Inc. in New York and London in 2005. The following quotations from pages 66-67, are relevant in the context of corporate governance:

"In the Twentieth Century the world saw a generation of non-totalitarian "nationalist" political leaders educated in the economic fallacies then dominant in the academic intelligentsia of Britain and elsewhere – that is to say regulationism."

"It is now largely accepted that the British economist, Peter Bauer, was right on the best approach to "Third World" poverty – as far as possible to give aid or assistance never to local governments or officials but to other recipients in states needing them."

"But worldwide, the problem is deeper. As Professor Deepaklal had pointed out in his Times Literary Supplement review of Bauer's last book, almost all of the long-advanced reasons for world poverty and most of the alleged cures for it are simply false. What we will see is aid that fails to reach the world's poor or else turns them into dependents, combined with a blaming of imperialism, colonialism or new-colonialism for what can be improved by more sensible methods."

Globalization, when not blocked by local politicians, has always benefited the population, reduced poverty and abated social evils. That is by no means to justify, for example, IMF mistakes over "capital account liberalization" let alone the errors of the Russian and other governments. But globalization, as such, does not warrant any of the moral or material criticism to be found among the doubtless well meaning but uncomprehending street walkers.

Such a profound and comprehensive review of previous policies and economic analysis will be difficult for many governments to accept, especially in respect of the "regulationism" prevalent at the centre of the European Union. The English speaking people must show the way – guided as always by the three hundred year old wisdom of Adam Smith.

———ᴏⱱᴈ———

COMPUTER TRANSLATIONS

IBM and other large American corporations found that they would not sell many computers if they did not provide translation programs. Now with a flick of a switch the owners of computers can print out documents in their own languages. Information from more than one hundred countries is now available in translation wherever someone is prepared to pay for it.

Chinese linguists soon found the way to translate all the languages of interest to them into pictograms. Mandarin is a dialect of Beijing which was adopted as an imperial and "universal" language but the calligraphy which unifies the country, no matter the dialect, is the pictogram. It is not a means of speaking but of understanding. Without the translation programs it would have been impossible for China to develop world wide trading and financial communications.

It is also difficult to see how the European Union could have legislated an incredibly complicated system of regulations without simultaneous translation both verbal and printed. Even greater problems would have arisen for the extended union of twenty-five language groups with perhaps more to come.

All of the countries of South America speak different languages, based on Spanish or Portuguese but still needing translation for continent-wide understanding.

The miracle of translation at the speed of light has enabled all countries to benefit from globalization, especially in respect of free trade. The world-wide creation of wealth can be expected to continue indefinitely. But there is another side to the picture.

Translation service can only be provided on an economic basis where there is sufficient demand. There are still six thousand languages in the process of disappearing and most of them cannot be saved by computers, even assuming massive international aid. How will those people trade with the rest of the world?

The acceptance of English as a second language would enable all language groups to become part of the world economy and to prosper, no matter how small their contribution may be to begin with. On the basis of minimum administrative costs they would make the most of their comparative advantages. Individuals will then be able to retain their spoken languages for as long as they wish.

The countries which can well afford translation services may adopt them primarily as a means of preserving their languages and not on the basis of economic analysis. Governments which discourage the use of English as a second language believe that their sovereignty would be threatened more by improved communications than by political union and the acceptance of common currencies. But in that they may be mistaken and subject to correction by a far sighted electorate and by an all-knowing world economy.

Translations which proceed one word or one phrase at a time may be adequate for simple commercial transactions but at more sophisticated levels of communication it may be impossible to convey precisely all of the subtleties of meaning by translations. In fact the message may be misunderstood whenever it is not in accordance with the existing mind-set of the receiver. That may be part of the reason for the rejection of Adam Smith's economic theories on the Continent of Europe. If free enterprise is not what they want they will probably interpret the information according to their predisposition. That cannot be blamed on any lack of skill by the translators.

In addition, translations from English documents are usually made by people whose native language is not English. An amusing letter was published in the Financial Times on February 28, 2006 which illustrates the potential for mis-translation which can destroy the entire purpose of the communication:

"Sir, I am intrigued to learn that Hans Günther Bollig's English is simpler than that of the native speakers he meets (Letters, February 24). He should come to Brussels, or at least read just about anything written in English by an official of the European Commission.

No one could accuse European Union English of being simple or easy to understand. It is stuffed with misused words like "modalities" (for "means" or "methods") and "service" (for department), not to mention barbaric coinages such as "subsidiarity" and "comitology". All self-respecting EU officials will write "of less importance" rather than "less important" and "during the process of the implementation of. . ." rather than "while implementing".

Long abstract nouns are always preferred to simple verb forms, and oddities such as "feedingstuffs" proliferate. Many older EU texts use US spelling, no doubt because US spelling was the default on official computers both before and for some time after the UK joined the EU.

None of this has much to do with native speakers. EU officials who are not native English speakers write in English as if it were their own language and, pace Mr. Bollig, Germans are among the worst offenders in this regard.

I advise him to read a few state aid decisions in English. Much translation into English is apparently not done by native speakers (at least, I hope not). My daily work involves turning the English of colleagues from other countries into something slightly more idiomatic and comprehensible – their writings are often inspired by EU texts, so I live surrounded by these horrors every day."

Sadly, many native speakers seem to accept them and even imitate them.

By the way, Mr. Bollig, I grew up as an illegitimate child in council housing – anyone who thinks there is still a tie-up between language and class in the UK is about 50 years out of date.

From Ms. Sasha Lewis.

The triumph of computerization has certainly extended the expectation of life for national sovereignty but other factors are working in the opposite direction. Time will tell.

CHAPTER TWENTY-SEVEN

—०৯১—

CIVILIZATION

The history of civilization is a patch-work quilt of spas-
modic cultural energy interspersed with political and
military activity which can only be described as uncivi-
lized. Some historians imply that outbursts of artistic genius somehow require a background of violence, cruelty,
religious intolerance and warfare because they occurred
at the same time. You do not have to believe that.

First, you must have the artists. No pope and no emperor and no king ever produced a work of art. Lucretia
Borgia never painted a picture.

Why batches of supreme artists, writers, philosophers and poets come and go so quickly is a mystery. No
amount of war or peace or government subsidy can find
them when they are not there. In the doldrums we have
to wait patiently for a fresh breeze.

The first tremulous steps towards civilization expressed the wish of many people to be civil to each other.
Without that they could not proceed with helping each
other in time of need; entertaining each other; presenting
their artistic efforts to an appreciative world; and planning to make life better instead of progressively worse
for everyone. To the extent that some people of genius

had conscious thoughts on these subjects, it was a global concept from the beginning.

The centuries of national sovereignty did not stop all progress in that direction. The challenge today is to make civilization more important than patriotism. We must set objectives that supersede the myopic views of national governments.

The volume of artefacts in museums built in the twenty first century or converted from disused power plants may well be greater than our inheritance of art from all previous generations. At the Tate Modern alone, London visitors spend many hours absorbing the work of thousands of artists, many of them exhibiting for the first time. They are not Rembrandt; they are not Leonardo da Vinci, they are not Michelangelo; they are not the Impressionists; they are not even Picasso.

Original? No. We are all standing on the shoulders of giants.

In the capital cities of the world are musicians who earn large sums of money whenever they strum a guitar or open their mouths to sing. But they are not Bach, Mozart, Beethoven or Chopin; they are not the choir of the Sistine Chapel; they are not the orchestra or the opera singers at the Scala Milano.

We have competent philosophers and architects, inheriting their skills from Ancient Greece. Not very much progress has been achieved in these matters in the meantime, except for building higher ivory towers. The danger inherent in worldwide computer communications is that instantaneous multiplicity will replace artistic creativity.

The intellectual capacity and the artistic perceptions of the English speaking people are no better and no worse than the average everywhere else. There is no necessity to succumb to pessimism but many of us do. That is the first enemy we have to defeat. The leaders of public opinion should pay careful attention to irrational impulses and mass reactions to temporary stimuli. So should we all. The danger of extreme divergence into incompatible and antagonistic groups is the last thing we want in the English speaking world. There is quite enough of that about elsewhere.

Fortunately we have a continuous inflow of new recruits from many different sources and widely different cultures. That should be sufficient to offset any tendencies we may have to contemplate our collective navel.

English speaking people are not simply the descendants of Celts, Saxons, Danes and Normans. They include everyone who can read and write in English and who expect to earn their living in English, at least partially. To begin with, that is the description of many millions of Chinese people in China, and elsewhere.

At $60 billion per year, China is the world's largest market for English language services, according to Mari Pearlman at ATS, an American group that developed TOEFL, a test of English language proficiency. Most of the dictionaries, text books and classroom aids are supplied by foreign companies in partnership with local firms. Macmillan has already sold more than 100 million textbooks in China, together with FLTRP which is the leading Chinese publisher of English-language books. Primary school pupils start to learn English at the age of nine, some at the age of six.

This is remarkable progress for a country which developed the concept of the nation state two thousand years before any European country existed. For an additional two thousand years the governments of Mainland China practised an extreme form of isolationism. They revelled in the delusion of national sovereignty and only now are they emerging from it.

Somehow we must find a way to convince the Chinese people that we greatly appreciate the contribution they are making to globalization and will do everything possible to follow their leadership, particularly in the matter of creating a world-wide communication system.

The number of Chinese car drivers will soon be equal to the entire population of the United States of America. They will drive because they can afford to buy a car, and that good fortune rose because they learned to develop world trade on the basis of the English language. That is what globalization means.

In India the people speak many dialects which are incomprehensible to each other but England provided centuries of government and education. The British Empire was not considered to be an unmitigated benefit but teaching children in elementary English schools has proved to provide a long-term advantage to the entire

population of India. All of the major cities and especially
the new Silicon Valley companies at Bangalore are able
to compete successfully with all of us in the English language. That competition is healthy for the whole world.
Pakistan is not very different.

On reflection we may come to the conclusion that
Europe is not very different either. Many mature people
and almost all of the young people involved in world
trade speak English perfectly well. They all use computers, which are designed and programmed in English
more or less worldwide. The international agencies in
Geneva are totally competent in English and so are the
main United Nations offices in New York. How could it
not be? Every member of UNO speaks his own language
but they all have to speak to each other. And of course
they are all highly educated. So, we may hope, are most
people in the bureaucracy of the European Union. IATA
has its headquarters in Montreal and no-one believes that
airlines could be directed and controlled in any other language than English.

It does not seem unrealistic to suppose that English is
already well advanced on the path to providing the world
with a global language. No-one else can make such a
claim. It will always be a second language for most people but that is all we are looking for.

Here and there a controversy arises concerning the
basic human right to preserve and use our own language
but in practice the economic cost of complete language
multiplication would be prohibitive. The members of the

European Union may well agree to keep all records in English and leave individual countries to translate any of their particular interests when they wish to do so; but that is more a pious hope than a prediction.

Newcomers to the language are always pleased to find that English literature does not consist only of the works of writers living in the British Isles. Every other country has produced great writers and they were all identified without delay, imported, translated and printed in England almost as soon as they were being read in their own countries. English scholars came from all over the world. They made translations from every country in Europe and beyond. As a result those books became part of English literature and are now available on the Internet. So in due course did books from North America, Australia, New Zealand, South Africa, the Caribbean and wherever English speaking people were reading and writing.

No other country has so many potential readers in one language. In fact for all other languages the readership is distinctly limited.

That is perhaps a depressing conclusion for people speaking only one language and that not English. But imagine that everyone could speak two languages, their own and English, what a better world that would be. What a more civilized world.

And without any government assistance we are well on the way to that happy situation. The survival and supremacy of English are not in question. There is no competition.

In poetry yes, because poetry cannot be translated. If you want to read Danté you have to learn Italian. If you do not understand a poetic allusion it is no use asking the poet what he meant. He can only say he is very sorry and try to write another poem. He cannot explain his poem in prose or by reference to anything else. Poetry is the best that can be done with a language; it is the highest art form.

The number of accepted poets who wrote in English is very large. Whether any who write today will survive indefinitely into the future is perhaps not so clear. Our descendants must wait and see. But the poetry we have inherited must be cherished if the quality of our language is to be preserved.

Shakespeare stands above everybody else who ever wrote plays or poetry. Nevertheless he is only part of our English genius. Somehow we must convince students that English is not simply a working language to assist us in the creation of wealth or for entertainment and recreational purposes. If we neglect any of the great works of prose or poetry we will all be the poorer for it, and so will the world.

But first, we must bring the world closer together by speaking English.

SUMMARY

In a free enterprise economy the exchange of goods and services will always be beneficial to both parties, otherwise it would not take place or would rapidly be discontinued. The same is true of trade between nations.

International trade, as with all economic activities, consists of costs and benefits. Governments impose taxes on the individuals and corporations which enjoy the trade, in order to cover the costs of maintaining law and order, providing infrastructure and supplying social services including health and welfare, education and training, which all contribute eventually to the creation of wealth.

In addition, governments may, if they wish, provide reimbursement to companies and individuals who suffer from competition, that is to say, the failed entrepreneurs. Usually governments favour producers rather than consumers although the electoral advantage from protecting minorities rather than majorities has never been clear.

The problem for governments is that if they divert revenue from profitable enterprises they will receive less tax revenue in future. This would also provide an incentive to profitable business to move away and if governments continued to divert revenue to unprofitable ventures they would force the profitable industries into bankruptcy if they did not relocate to more appreciative authorities.

The policy which would best ensure the long term interest of each nation would be to accept the verdict of the free market and provide retraining and relocation of employees from loss-making industries to areas of greater economic advantage, when compared with overseas competitors.

Globalization describes the progress towards one world; an ever-deepening economic integration; a common means of communication; compatible laws; and a reduction of the motivation of nation states to restrict freedom of expression and freedom of movement across borders. No single state can deal effectively with worldwide threats to security such as terrorism, global warming, mass epidemics or national disasters; so cooperation between nations is essential if they want their populations to prosper.

It is in the self-interest of all countries to come to terms with this new reality. The economic and social improvement of everyone depends on worldwide progress together.

A major obstacle to globalization is national sovereignty, the belief of national governments that they are uniquely competent to respond to the requirements of their electorates and do not need any assistance from anyone else. They are all mistaken in that delusion. But, it must be admitted, even national sovereignty would be better than a tyrannical world government.

Centrally organized international agencies already exist but they cannot impose taxes on the world community. World government is not a practical proposition. Taxes must continue to be imposed and distributed at the nation state, provincial and municipal levels, according to the priorities of each community, preferably decided on the basis of representative democracy.

The only hope we have of progress towards globalization is that national and local governments will be persuaded by their electorates to permit and encourage the greatest possible creation of wealth. The whole world will then have the opportunity to participate in the enjoyment of benefits provided by the economic organizations which succeed. That will provide the greatest possible tax revenue for governments to distribute according to their own priorities, provided they refrain from activity designed to restrict the progress of globalization.

The possibility of the renunciation by governments of their sovereign pretensions appears to most people to be slight. The countries with the best prospects of resolving their own problems and the problems of the rest of the world are the English Speaking People for a variety of historical reasons, including a superior economic theory, and above all because English has no competition in the development of a world language.

English Speaking People will be acting in their own self-interest, as Adam Smith always said. But we have a responsibility to the rest of the world to do it well and to do it soon.

As John Dryden wrote:
We must bear witness before we die
That things are not otherwise, but thus.